WHO'S GONNA LOVE ME?

DON KIMBALL

■

VALENCIA, CALIFORNIA   ALLEN, TEXAS

Credits

Special Consultant: Karen Fisher
Book Design: Cheryl Carrington
Cover and Interior Photos: Peter Crossman
Cover Color: Richard Blair

Copyright © 1988 by Tabor Publishing, a division of DLM, Inc.

All rights reserved. No part of this book shall be reproduced or transmitted in any form or by any means, electronic or mechanical, including photocopying, recording, or by any information or retrieval system, without written permission from the Publisher.

Send all inquiries to:
Tabor Publishing
25115 Avenue Stanford, Suite 130
Valencia, California 91355

A

Presentation

Printed in the United States of America
ISBN 0-89505-769-7

1 2 3 4 5   92 91 90 89 88

Contents

Introduction		5
1	**A Day in the Life**	6
2	**Slabs of Concrete**	20
3	**Look in the Mirror**	48
4	**Love without Strings**	70
5	**Party God!**	96
6	**Truth and Consequences**	120
7	**Who Me? A Lover?**	138
8	**Let the Fun Begin!**	162
Who Am I Gonna Love?		173

INTRODUCTION

Sure, everybody tells you that you can make it! Everybody says it's just a phase. But you are really scared. There is a lot of pressure on you. What will you become? Who will you be? Who (if anybody) will love you?

If these feelings and questions are important to you, then this book is important to you. I want you to be the best you can be! I have been where you are. I spend my life being with teenagers. I know you, your music, your culture, your feelings, and your fears. In this book, I will help you face those fears. I will help you get in touch with yourself, your friends, your teachers, even your parents. I will help you face the toughest of all questions—"Who's gonna love me?"

1

A Day in the Life

■

- Everybody's on my case—even me!
- If one more person tells me I am on a journey, I swear I'll scream!
- What are friends for, anyway?
- Why is everybody so confused?

WHO'S GONNA LOVE ME?

Sometimes life is no darn good! Whoever had the idea of forcing people to go through all this just to become an adult should be shot. There has got to be an easier way!

Some days are pretty good—even lots of fun. But then there are days when everything falls apart. There we are again—wondering what it's all about.

Take my friend Jesse, for example.

Jesse hangs out in his car at lunch while he listens to his Nakamichi. He's got a power amplifier, two twelve-inch subwoofers, twelve mids and tweeters, and over a thousand watts per channel at his disposal. It's his great escape on wheels.

One day, he's sitting there, eating nachos. Here come Cindy and Linda. Jesse really likes Cindy. So when he sees them, he shoves the nachos aside. (He is thankful that the huge zit he discovered this morning is on the left side of his jaw. Cindy won't see it from the passenger seat.) Cindy and Linda climb in.

> And that was U2 closing out our commercial-free half hour on KULT. Kelly Fitzgerald is standing by in the newsroom. How 'bout it, Fitz?

"Hey, we just missed U2!" pouts Cindy. Jesse isn't sure if Cindy comes around to be with him or just to be with his stereo. But Jesse answers anyway.

A DAY IN THE LIFE

"I've got the tape," he says. His voice cracks. (Oh, no!) Linda giggles. Jesse's face turns bright red. Jesse feels the hot rush of blood to his ears. His heart has been racing the whole time. He hisses at himself in his head: *Cool, idiot! You got to be cool!*

> Thanks, Doug. In the news, Denver County Court today arraigned a twenty-two-year-old gang member for the Capitol Hill murder. Matthew "C.C." Vick is accused in the golf-club beating death of fifty-three-year-old Harriet Lawyer-Duvallo last Tuesday. Vick was a member of the Rolling 30 Crips gang in Los Angeles before moving to Denver. Three other gang members from Los Angeles are under arrest in connection with the crime.

Jesse reaches for his tape box, but Cindy grabs his arm to stop him. Now his heart is really racing. "Let's just listen to the news. I gotta know some current events for social studies class next hour."

Just then, Roger (Linda's boyfriend) climbs into the back seat. Jesse doesn't really like Roger—he's always putting on a show. But Jesse doesn't think he has the guts to challenge Roger. Roger is kind of a leader in their circle of friends, and Jesse feels like he's on the fringe with that group as it is. Besides, Linda and Cindy are best friends. So, Jesse doesn't say anything to Roger.

WHO'S GONNA LOVE ME?

Roger doesn't say anything, either. He just starts making out with Linda. (Geez!)

> Testimony continues today in the murder trial of seventeen-year-old Sean Sellers, accused of killing his mother and stepfather. The youth is believed to have been involved in satanic practices which led to the murders. In testimony today, classmates claimed he carried around vials of fresh blood and drank from them in the lunchroom.

"Ooooh, gross!" Cindy acts like she really cares. Jesse's worried that Roger and Linda will think Cindy is calling *them* gross. He glances at the rearview mirror. Instead, he catches Roger's eye. "Take a picture, man!" Roger is such a great guy!

Jesse sinks down in his seat. (The face goes bright red again.) Why did Roger have to say that in front of Cindy? Jesse stares straight ahead, hanging onto the steering wheel, wishing everybody'd just leave him alone. Just a few minutes ago, Jesse daydreamed about asking Cindy out. Now, he is sure he doesn't stand a chance with her.

> A pregnant teenager from Lafayette was found dead in her parents' garage this morning, an apparent victim of suicide. She left death notes for her parents and her boyfriend, but the contents have not yet been revealed. Funeral services for Katy Albrite, sixteen, will be held Thursday.

A DAY IN THE LIFE

Katy Albrite. Jesse knew a Katy Albrite. They had gone to grade school together before Katy's family moved away. Could it be the same person?

"If I got pregnant, I'd kill my boyfriend, not myself." Cindy tries to make light of the story, and Jesse just tries to lighten up. But his smile (and his usual witty crack) is buried under the weight of the news. Katy Albrite.

The school bell announces the end of lunch period. Cindy, Roger, and Linda go flying off to their next class. But Jesse just sits there. *Suicide.* Katy actually did it. "I am not that brave!" Jesse says—out loud.

Who cares about this life anyway? It's so stupid. Trying to impress girls—trying to be cool—trying to fit in! Who cares? Cindy probably thinks he's a jerk now. Roger never liked him anyway. What's the point?

Jesse trudges to his next class in a daze. Emotional overload! He just feels numb, like a robot on low batteries. He walks into class unaware that the late bell has already rung. He takes a seat by the door.

Whap! Mr. Sandstrom's pointer smacks down on Jesse's desk. Jesse flinches—the class laughs. "Glad you could join us, Mr. Nolan. Do you plan to turn in your assignment?"

Jesse starts flipping through his book, but he's not really paying attention to what he's doing. His anger does a power surge. "What right does this fungus brain have to treat me like this?

Why does Sandstrom have to make me the butt of the class's laughter? What does Sandstrom know about what I am going through today? Not a damn thing! And where's the dumb assignment? Oh, forget it! Just forget it!"

All of a sudden, Jesse's math book slams into the chalkboard. He's not quite sure how that happened, but he is standing now, glaring at Mr. Sandstrom. Tears are coming to his eyes. He quickly grabs his other books and runs out of the classroom.

Jesse needs help. Oh, he's not crazy. And what he's just gone through isn't all that unusual. But he needs to understand what's happening to him. He's angry with Roger for the putdown. (Should have kicked Roger's butt—or so he feels!) He's embarrassed about the way he acted in front of Cindy. He's angry with Linda. He's angry with Mr. Sandstrom. He feels stupid about his behavior in class. And Katy's death has rubbed his nose in his own fear of death and his fear of life. Jesse is one big emotional overload. Bailout!

Everybody is on Jesse's case—most especially Jesse!

ANOTHER JOURNEY?

Is Jesse alone in this experience? Or have you felt some of those same feelings? Have you ever gotten to a point where nothing makes sense

A DAY IN THE LIFE

anymore? Nothing goes right. No one treats you right. And no one understands what you're feeling.

You're not alone. Did you know that most high schoolers think they're going crazy at some time or another? "Gee, I'm weird! How do I deal with all that I'm experiencing and feeling? Where can I hide? How can I make it through all this stuff? And not just make it through, but find out why it's worth going through this? What makes life worth living? Who has the answers?"

So you picked up (or were given) this book, and you hope to find some answers here. You know that there are books out there with answers: *Fifteen Steps to a Better You* or *How to Be Happy All the Time* or *The Fast and Easy Way to Achieve Your Potential*.

The bad news is, this is not one of those books.

The good news is, I'm not going to make any dumb promises to you. Not that the people who write those books are liars. It's just that they've tried to make simple and clean something that is complicated and messy.

On the surface, it seems nice to have fifteen easy-to-follow steps. People like to be able to measure their progress. In school, you feel like a better person the closer you get to graduation, the better your grades are, the more varsity badges you have, the higher your chair in the trumpet section, and the more offices you hold in clubs.

WHO'S GONNA LOVE ME?

If life could be measured in the same way school achievement is, if life could be boiled down to fifteen steps, then you'd know how you were doing by which step you were on. You could compare your progress with your peers' progress. You'd know where you stand. "Mom! Dad! Guess what? I got a B+ in *life!*"

Then what? What happens when you reach step fifteen? Do you graduate? Live happily ever after? Repeat the steps? Die? Why stick around another seventy years?

Life isn't a series of steps. And life does not come with a set of instructions. The Creator did not pass out an owner's manual and a warranty card to each baby born. Life is just as complicated as you think it is. And that makes the process of living really challenging. That makes life worth living!

I suppose life is a journey. (I know how tired you are of hearing that!) But it is not the kind of journey you're used to. "Take a left turn at the next stoplight, and it will be the third building on the right!" I don't see too many people handing out maps for life, do you?

I am not giving you steps or maps! If life is a journey, it is a funny one—one where you have to wander around bumping into other people. So, instead of steps, I'm going to write about people and relationships.

Jesse had a relationship with Cindy—with Roger and with Mr. Sandstrom. There was a relationship between C.C. Vick and the woman he killed. Katy Albrite and her boyfriend had a relationship that killed Katy! And I will be writing about you and your relationships—with yourself, your parents, other adults, your friends, and (believe it or not) God.

WHAT ARE FRIENDS FOR?

Why focus on relationships? Think about it. When you're worried about grades, is it because of the grades themselves? Or is it because of how you'll feel about yourself, and how your parents will feel about you if you goof up?

When you spend hours getting ready for a dance, is it because you are a perfectionist? Or do you want to impress your friends? When Jesse threw his book against the chalkboard, was he angry about the assignment? Or was he angry with Mr. Sandstrom for not understanding?

When you're most happy, it's because of the good stuff that is happening in your relationships. And when you're hurting the most, it's because something is wrong in those same relationships.

When you feel what Jesse was feeling, you may wonder if relationships are really worth it. Wouldn't life be simpler if everyone joined monasteries? Or related only to computers?

People could get in their own little boxes. Robots could serve their meals, exercise with them, and do their chores. People would spend

WHO'S GONNA LOVE ME?

the day writing computer programs or watching MTV or reading books. No one could touch them! No one could hurt them! No one could embarrass them! No one would *ever* hurt or die!

Of course, there'd also be no one to hang out with. No one to love. No one to share your joys with. No one to break the routine. No one to stop your loneliness.

And since the only way to get to God is through relationships, you'd have to find new ways to experience God's power and presence. When God created the universe, everything was good—*everything*. The heavens, the earth, the light, the sky, the land, the moon and the stars, the trees, the creatures, people—everything was good. The very first thing God recognized that was *not* good? (The truth!) "God said: 'It is *not good* to be alone.'"

SO WHAT'S THE PROBLEM?

Relationships tell you how happy or how sad you are. They're the reasons you feel good about life or bad about life. They're the reasons you like yourself or hate yourself. Relationships bring joy, confusion, happiness, turmoil, grief, peace, and fulfillment. You grow—in body, mind, and even spirit—through your relationships. The strange and wonderful way human beings are made gives life meaning in *relationships*. Period!

A DAY IN THE LIFE

Now, you might be getting quite a different message about relationships! Teachers rarely talk about relationships. They are big on *information*. You probably feel that your job is to acquire tons of information and to spit it back out in the proper order. Fail here, and you don't go to college—you don't get a good job—you don't amount to anything! All that relationship stuff? Well, teenagers can pick that up on their own.

Even most parents find it easier to talk about information than about relationships. They have no trouble explaining chores to you or discussing your grades with you. But try asking your father about dating and sex, and you might hear, "Ask your mother." Then your mother looks the other way and says, "Ask your father." And there you are. You will be taught more about driving a car than about relationships.

Hey, I'm not blaming teachers or parents. They were raised in an information society, too. And with computers, you can get any information you want—anytime you want. With radio, television, magazines, and in a million other ways, information is thrown at you every waking hour—from all directions.

So, is it a surprise that people look for life's answers in soaps, talk-show shrinks, books, techniques, and formulas? Society's big promise is that the answers can be found there.

Well, my friend, I am making a different kind of promise to you. Learn to relate to others,

WHO'S GONNA LOVE ME?

and you'll find true happiness. (Give me a break!) I'm serious! I'm talking about the kind of happiness that allows you to feel good—even about feeling bad.

I could write a book full of "baloney" for you. But I know that you have heard too much of that already. I could give you a lot of information, but information makes sense only if there are real relationships—real experiences—behind it.

I could tell you that it hurts to have a best friend move away. You could even say, "Yeah, I'll buy that." But it's only after a friend really moves away that *you* feel the pain. The experience makes the information meaningful. Information is *about* experience. It can't replace experience. It can help experience. But it isn't a substitute.

So instead of just writing *about* life, I want to muck around in life with you. I want to talk about real relationships and how they hit you. I want to look at teenage relationships, parent-teen relationships, adult-teen relationships, and (here's that word again) God-teen relationships.

I'm even thinking about looking at relationships in the Bible. The Bible (believe it or not) is a collection of stories about relationships—God's relationships with Adam, Eve, Noah, Abraham, David, Solomon—the whole gang. The Bible has stories about family feuds, wars, love affairs, political campaigns, and long quests. (These are all relationship events!)

A DAY IN THE LIFE

The Bible is full of love, hate, jealousy, fear, longing, sacrifice, kindness, desire—and a million other *relationship* qualities. In fact, the bottom line in the Bible is God's *relationship* with people. And God gets pretty personal—so personal that God crawled right inside human flesh in Jesus. (That's personal!) So, if I pick out some Bible stuff, it is because it really fits.

Are you ready? Remember, I have no fifteen easy steps—no pat answers. Just relationships! And lurking along the way is a better understanding of yourself, others, and God.

Interested?

Scared?

Feel like hiding?

Please, don't! I'll be going right along with you.

2

Slabs of Concrete

■

- Am I really a square peg in a world full of round holes?
- So, what do I have to give up?
- I am comfortable right where I am!
- (Shh, don't tell anybody.) I'm scared stiff!
- I haven't got time for the pain!

WHO'S GONNA LOVE ME?

The homecoming pep rally—what a trip! The football team is being introduced—one by one. The cheerleaders are jumping up and down, waving their pom-poms. (Each one shakes a little more when her boyfriend is announced.) The drama kids are pointing and laughing at the cheerleaders. The pep band members (who would rather be jamming than playing fight songs) are slumped in their chairs. They're clapping but just barely, and are doing their best to look bored. The druggies are standing on the bleachers and whooping it up. They are high—but not on school spirit.

Now take a closer look. John is laughing it up with all the drama kids. But he feels a little funny. One of those cheerleaders is Jenny. She and he were buddies back in the sixth grade. Not that Jenny is any less guilty of abandoning the relationship than John. They have both found different groups of friends that enjoy the same things they do. And (of course) they don't associate with people from other groups. That's the way it is with special groups—with *cliques.*

Meantime, Jenny can't stop worrying about her period being late. So, she covers up her fears, and she cheers extra loud when Todd is introduced. She didn't even enjoy sex, but when you're dating the starting quarterback, you just don't say no.

Jenny has worked hard to make it as a cheerleader. And her relationship with Todd is deeply affected by her relationship with the other cheerleaders. The fact that she's dating him at all (and not a drama kid or druggie) is because of her clique.

Her friends know how to keep a guy. If you love a guy, and he loves you, you show your love by having sex. Don't you?

Michele is hoping the team wins tomorrow, but instead of cheering she studies the keys on her clarinet. The football players are a bunch of dumb jocks anyway. Michele has learned to hate jocks after being ignored by them for years. She can see right through their games. She's playing a different game. She just waits for a jock to do something stupid so that she and her friends can talk about how dumb he is. Her clique finds unity in rejecting the people they've been rejected by.

Willy feels pretty good. He's got a good buzz on. He's trying to figure a good excuse for getting home late. He won't let his mom slap him around again for drinking. Willy has found a clique that helps him deal with the pain his mom causes. He uses alcohol and drugs to numb that pain. Other people in his circle of friends use alcohol or drugs just to belong.

THE NEED TO BELONG

Everyone needs to belong. Even loners need to belong. They drift from group to group and try to find a place where they fit in. Or maybe they don't drift at all anymore. They just criticize all groups—to cover up the sharp pain of not belonging. They (maybe more than anybody) still have the need.

The need to belong is pretty basic stuff. It's not just a need for teenagers. It's a need for all people. The need to belong is right up there with some other pretty big needs.

First is the need for physical survival—food, water, and shelter meet that need. A starving kid in Ethiopia isn't too worried about belonging. That kid is completely occupied with getting a scrap of food.

The next big need is for safety—protection from enemies, personal security, a sense that you won't be completely wiped out. If you are staring down the barrel of a gun in a dark alley, *belonging* is the farthest thing from your mind. But you need to feel *emotionally* safe, too. You need to feel sure that nobody is going to hurt your *feelings*.

The number three need *is* belonging! Right after survival and preservation is the need to feel a part of something—the need for affection.

Now, *most* people in North America have little problem meeting the first two basic needs. If you had the money to spend on this book, I'll bet you're not worried about getting food or water. Physical safety is a concern, but for the most part, we are pretty safe people.

So, the first needs that grab you are emotional safety and the need to belong. So, you

SLABS OF CONCRETE

look for a group to belong to where you are not going to be hurt emotionally. Most people come equipped with a family—sort of a "built-in group." That doesn't mean that the family is always safe, but it is a place to start.

If your family suddenly falls on hard times, and you really don't know where your next meal is coming from, you probably won't worry too much about belonging. Your time and energy will be occupied with the more basic needs of hunger and thirst. If your mother or father is an alcoholic, or is abusive, or if your family comes apart, then belonging and emotional safety become very, very important. But by now you are looking for groups to belong to that are outside your family. That is great! That is the way it is supposed to be!

But how do you meet the need to belong? Cliques can meet that need. They provide emotional safety (sort of). But the price of belonging to a closed group is pretty steep. You are safe in that group only if you fit in with their rules—all of them.

The Cost of Belonging

What price are you willing to pay to belong? Are you willing to dress a certain way? Are you willing to talk a certain way? How about music? How about your *attitude?*

John, Jenny, Michele, and Willy have all developed styles that fit into their cliques. I

WHO'S GONNA LOVE ME?

haven't given you much of a description of these four, but I'd bet you could tell me about them. (Go ahead—try!) Focus on three areas—clothes, music, and attitude toward school.

Now compare your thoughts with my descriptions. Start with John. Remember him? He belongs to the drama group.

- *Clothes:* Weird, by most people's standards. He's trying to make a statement with his clothes. And that statement is "Hey, I'm different!"
- *Music:* Anything that's slightly away from the popular trend.
- *Attitude toward school:* English, art, and music teachers are cool. The others are dumb. They don't see the artistic side of life. They are *boring*.

Next there is Jenny—the cheerleader who is worried about being pregnant. She has a pretty strong drive to belong.

- *Clothes:* Anything that is *in*. She gets her wardrobe right off the pages of *Seventeen!*
- *Music:* Straight Top 40. (Surprised?)
- *Attitude toward school:* School is just a stepping-stone to a career (or something). Don't *learn* anything, but get good grades—at any cost.

How about Michele. Remember her? At the rally, she was fooling around with her clarinet.

SLABS OF CONCRETE

- *Clothes:* Last year's fashions—even hand-me-downs from her sister.
- *Music:* Oh, she does listen to the Top 40 a lot. But she really likes jazz and classical. That stuff really lifts her up and carries her away.
- *Attitude toward school:* Do your very best. Get the most out of every class. Grades are good, but learning is better.

Then there's Willy. He was sky-high, remember, standing at the top of the bleachers—watching the world spin around.

- *Clothes:* Beat-up army jacket, torn-up jeans (or fatigues), a worn black T-shirt, and boots.
- *Music:* Heavy metal. Period.
- *Attitude toward school:* "It sucks!"

Why? Because druggies, populars, band kids, and drama kids behave *to belong!* They dress to belong. They listen to the music that *shows* they belong. They even get an attitude toward school that fits the group. They are willing to sacrifice almost anything (even their own individuality) just to belong!

The Big If!

When you search for belonging, your goal is to find love. Love includes finding safety and belonging. But you can't stop there. In cliques

WHO'S GONNA LOVE ME?

(heck, in a whole lot of human relationships), real love is nowhere to be found. The relationships get stuck at safety and belonging, and never move on to real love.

So, what is love?

First, I'd like to do something most English teachers really hate. I want to talk about what love is *not*. Maybe I can do this best with a story. (Hang in there with me!)

In the seventh grade, Kim joined the band as a drummer. She really liked the other band members and quickly became a member of their group—their clique. The band kids were mostly good students, sometimes teacher's pets. Most of them didn't smoke or drink. Kim pretty much fit that mold.

But Kim was very curious about other people's groups—other people's styles. She rode the bus with some kids who weren't really into school. One day her neighbor invited her to a party—during school hours. (Sounded like fun—in a scary kind of way.) Well, Kim skipped a couple classes. At the party, Kim had a few sips of beer (which she didn't like at all). She took a drag off someone's cigarette. (Yuk!) Kim chalked the whole thing up to experience and forgot about it.

End of story? No way! Kim's "friends" didn't forget. Word got out among the band kids that Kim was a *burnout*. So, some of the leaders of the clique decided not to hang out with Kim anymore. And the rest followed along.

SLABS OF CONCRETE

Kim had broken an unspoken agreement with the band kids. She was accepted *if* she did what they did, and *if* she didn't do what they didn't do. Now, she no longer belonged because her behavior didn't fit the group's behavior.

Kim had discovered the *BIG IF*. Oh sure, she was accepted, but only under certain conditions. The group's acceptance had strings attached. "We will accept you *if* you wear what we wear, *if* you listen to our music, *if* you talk the way we talk, *if* you like the people we like and don't like the people we don't like, and *if* you behave the way we behave." (So there!)

You don't even have to *hear* the word *if*. As a matter of fact, most people don't come right out and state their conditions for acceptance. Instead, they drop hints. Try these statements on for size. They all have hidden *ifs*.

- "What're you hanging around *him* for?" *(If* you like the people we like . . .)
- "I can't believe she's listening to *that stupid* music." *(If* you listen to the music we listen to . . .)
- "What do you mean, you're not going to the party? Everyone is going to be there." *(If* you do the things we do . . .)

Have you heard your friends say anything like that lately? Have *you* said anything like that lately to someone else? Whenever you go around attaching *ifs* to your friends, the relationships have strings attached.

WHO'S GONNA LOVE ME?

This is *not* love. Using the *big if* with the word *love* downgrades love into plain old acceptance. Only you know for sure how many of your relationships are based on conditional acceptance.

Test It Yourself

It's easy to see that Kim's friends were accepting her conditionally and not really loving her. You can probably look back on some of your junior high friendships and see that they had a lot of *ifs* attached to them. But what about the friends you have now? Sure, you do things the same way they do, but that's because you *like* to do things *their* way. (Don't you?) But do your friends like you only because you fit in?

There is one way to find out. Do something that doesn't fit their mold. Pick something big (by group standards), and do it more than once. Now where do you stand with your friends?

Would druggies hang around someone who has stopped doing drugs? How long would "trendies" hang around with somebody who got a radical haircut? (I mean really radical!) How long would the sports crowd tolerate somebody who hung out with the band kids? And so on, and so on, and so on. If you started hanging around with a different crowd (especially a crowd that your group picks on), how long would you have before the group starts rejecting you?

SLABS OF CONCRETE

Kim left the band kids and became a druggie in high school. She learned to like alcohol and cigarettes—and drugs. For a while, she was a B student, but she hid that fact from her new friends.

During her junior year, Kim even let her grades slip some. Or maybe they slipped because she was high most of the time. At any rate, by spring of her junior year, Kim wasn't very happy with herself. She was tired of the routine—going to school, getting high, trying to act normal in front of teachers, and coming up with excuses instead of homework assignments.

She wanted more out of life. (She really did.) Well, her older sister, whom Kim liked, suggested she go on a retreat. Kim went, and (guess what?) she loved it. Kim felt loved and accepted by the people she met on the retreat.

But this would never do! Kim's druggie friends couldn't understand why she had changed. They didn't want her around unless she was going to get high with them. Kim's new friends from the retreat expected her to leave her old friends behind and stay straight.

Once again, Kim had broken the code of belonging. The druggies accepted her when she was a druggie—when she got high with them. The retreat gang accepted her when she acted holy—when she was clean.

Kim needed to belong. She feared giving up the comfortable old relationships that she had with the druggies. But she also didn't want to give up the possibility of new friends, a new place to belong, and a different way to live.

Kim was like the middle person in a trapeze act—tossed between two groups. She couldn't grab hold of the new group unless she let go of the old. She feared letting go. She feared that awful time of tumbling in midair, and she wasn't completely certain that the new group would even catch her.

In the end, Kim got off the trapeze altogether. Since she belonged in neither group, she hung out with the few friends in both groups that accepted her for who she was.

That's how that story really ended with Kim. (Kind of a letdown, isn't it?) But then, how would you have wanted it to end?

FEAR

A whole lot of groups are not based on love. (Not too many of the groups Kim got stuck with really cared about Kim.) Many groups—especially cliques—are based on fear. They reveal their fears in their unspoken *ifs*.

Fear operates in all relationships (at least a little bit). But in some relationships, fear can get pretty big. Katy Albrite (remember, the pregnant teenager?) feared the rejection of her boyfriend. She feared the pain that she and her parents would go through. She feared life as a pregnant teenager even more than she feared death.

SLABS OF CONCRETE

There are many types of fear. For now I'd like to look at three of the most basic fears—fear of rejection, fear of pain, and fear of failure. (There is another *really big* fear—the fear of death. But I'll save that for later.) Each of these three fears operates in some of the relationships you have in your life right now.

Fear of Rejection

Kevin felt he had walked seven miles in the last hour—just pacing. He knows Meg is sitting with her girlfriends at the fast-food place at the end of the mall. He pictures her sipping on a Coke, laughing with her friends, tossing her head back with her auburn hair flowing down her back.

"What's the big deal?" he thinks. "Guys have been doing this for centuries. What's the worst thing that could happen? She'll come up with some excuse for turning me down. And that'll be it! Okay, I'm ready."

Kevin strides confidently down the mall. "This is it! This is it! I am finally going to do it." He feels a rush. His heart is pounding. His palms are just a little damp.

He walks into the restaurant. There is Meg—just like he pictured her. She is with Sandy (that awful Sandy) and Helen and Carrie.

Sandy spots Kevin first and whispers something to Meg. Meg looks down. She seems to be fiddling with something in her purse. The girls go on talking, but they are all aware of Kevin.

WHO'S GONNA LOVE ME?

"Meg, could I talk to you for a second?" Kevin says. (His mouth is like sandpaper.) Meg looks at Sandy (who rolls her eyes slightly—enough for Kevin to notice). Kevin senses that things are not going well. Well, too late now! Meg slides out of the booth and walks a few feet away with Kevin.

"Meg," starts Kevin. (He is starting to lose it.) "Would you . . . er . . . could you? Ah, I was thinking . . ."

"What do you want, Ke*vin?*" pushes Meg. (How he hates it when people say "Ke*vin*" like that!)

"Meg . . . , well . . ." That was it! "Meg, could I use your notes from Thursday's lit class? I lost mine." (What a jerk!)

This is fear of rejection at work. Kevin really wants to ask Meg to a movie. But if she says no, Kevin is rejected. He just can't face that. He is so scared Meg will reject him that he changes his mind in midstream. The risk was just too big for Kevin to take. (Of course, he feels like a jerk afterward.)

I want to offer myself in a relationship. But I expect to be turned down. So, I'd just as soon not offer myself at all. I won't even try. I stop dead in my tracks.

But sometimes I do something even worse. I take out some rejection insurance. I wear a *mask* so that I look like somebody you *won't* reject. How could you reject me? In my mask, I am just like you want me to be.

SLABS OF CONCRETE

In a university study, some professors found out that junior high girls seem to let their grades drop to gain the approval of boys. The girls don't want to risk rejection by boys. (They are new at the boy thing.) And they believe boys like dumb girls better. So the girls put on the "dumb" mask. The study showed that when their grades dropped, the girls actually felt better about themselves. (Weird? Well, not really!)

Some girls wear the "dumb" mask well into high school. All of a sudden, they find themselves scrambling to graduate or get into college. But, hey! The girls aren't the only mask wearers. Boys like to wear the mask of "no emotions." They learn this pretty young. Big boys don't cry, right? So, the emotions are hidden behind a tough mask.

People hide some of their best qualities behind a mask. Intelligence, true feelings, morals, beliefs, attitudes, and taste—all these and many more are covered up out of fear of rejection.

Did you know that there are closet music listeners? Maybe you're one of them. They listen to the music their group likes when they're with their friends. But the minute they get home, they close the door and listen to the kind of music *they* like. The fear of rejection keeps them from admitting to their friends what they enjoy. (This is not all that crazy. The fear of rejection is strong.)

How many romances have been crushed by the fear of rejection? Kevin is *not* the only guy

WHO'S GONNA LOVE ME?

to be afraid to ask a girl out. There are a lot of masks worn to get relationships going between boys and girls. Sometimes people even end up *marrying* the mask instead of the person. Then things get really rough. The very basis for the relationship is false. And all this happens because of the fear of rejection.

Another thing—fear of rejection keeps relationships on the surface. Oh, we can talk about the weather or that tough history exam. We can even talk about people we agree to dislike—people from other cliques. But I'll never tell you about me. I won't reveal the person behind the mask. You won't have the chance to reject me because I am not going to give you the chance to know me.

The funny thing about rejection—masks don't always help. You can be rejected anyway—masks or no masks, games or no games. Kim was rejected by the band kids for being herself. But think about it! Haven't you ever heard something like, "What does she see in him? He is such a fake!"

Here's the point. Rejection can happen anyway, so you might just as well be yourself. Scary thought? I know, it's easier to be rejected for being fake. Then you can always say, "Oh, they're just rejecting my mask, they're not really rejecting me." On the other hand, they're also *believing* in your mask, and not in you.

Probably the worst thing about the fear of rejection is that it causes more rejection. Like

Michele and her band friends rejecting the jocks, the attitude becomes "I'll reject you before I get rejected." All too often, true and honest acceptance is never even given a chance.

Fear of Pain

It happened again last night. Debbie had spent hours getting ready for this date. Ron is one of the neatest guys in school—cute, funny, athletic, intelligent, a little shy. But he had asked *Debbie* out (not Missy or Barbara or any of Debbie's other popular friends). He asked her.

The date was wonderful. Ron was relaxed, and that helped Debbie loosen up. They laughed about Mrs. Schulte's antics in English class and groaned about the recent midterms. He talked about his dream of becoming an Air Force pilot, and she talked about her struggles in choosing a college. Her eyes sparkled when she laughed, he said. He held her hand as they walked around the lake. His good-night kiss at the door was gentle—not too aggressive. This was *the best!*

Then the porch light snapped on, and Debbie's heart sank. The door flew open, and Dad boomed, "C'mon in. I've got some hot chocolate to end your evening." Ron accepted the invitation—completely unaware of the fate that awaited him.

Dad started the conversation innocently enough. "Do you think the baseball team can snap that losing streak?" said Dad—all smiles.

WHO'S GONNA LOVE ME?

"I hear you're on the track team," Dad went on. "How do you think you'll do in the state meet?"

Then dear old Dad started in with the *ultimate* questions—some real zingers. "Your coach is a member of our church. Do you go to church? Which church? Is your faith important to you? What *is* important to you? Do you plan to go to college? What are you going to do with your life?"

In fifteen minutes, what had started to be such a great evening collapsed right in front of Debbie's eyes. She hurt so bad she wanted to scream.

Ron went from composed to challenged to shocked to angry to defeated. He left without a word. And Debbie ran to her room, not sure whether she wanted to kill her dad or just cry herself to death.

Debbie's dad wasn't trying to hurt his daughter. In fact, he was trying to do just the opposite—save *her* from being hurt. He was operating out of his *fear of pain*. He couldn't stand the thought of some guy breaking Debbie's heart. He didn't want her to hurt, and he didn't want to hurt right along with her.

So (probably without thinking), he acted on his fear of pain. But he ended up causing more pain for Debbie. That's the way fear works. You try to avoid something, and end up causing the very thing you fear. Fear of pain may even cause someone to inflict pain.

SLABS OF CONCRETE

Fear of pain affects your relationship with your parents. Sometimes it is only the fear of a hassle. Your parents nag you. They do things that irritate you. They don't understand when you try to communicate with them.

So, you give up. You choose not to deal with the hassle of being with them. You don't want to be in a relationship with them when it starts to cost you something.

Fear of pain operates a lot in teenage relationships. Guys dump their pregnant girlfriends because they don't want to deal with the pain *they've helped cause!* Friends avoid talking about another friend's parents' divorce because they really don't want to share the pain their friend is feeling. Even best friends may ignore hints of suicide because suicide is just too painful to confront.

By now you might have figured out that fear of pain keeps people from going deeper into a relationship. Maybe you have gotten past the fear of rejection enough to reveal yourself to another person. You are able to share some joys and concerns. But you can't share the other person's pain. (You can't even share your own.)

You learn pretty early from your friends, your parents, and other adults that pain is something to be avoided. If no one will be with you while you hurt, then hurting must be bad. Society tells you the same thing. If you hurt, take a painkiller. Don't look at the cause of the pain. Just get rid of the pain. There is a problem with this. If the cause of the pain isn't discovered, the pain keeps coming back.

Now, nobody *likes* pain. But when it comes to relationships, fear of pain can stop real love dead. Nobody can love without some pain. That is a fact. But society would like you to believe all pain is bad. So, if you can't handle the pain, numb it. Cover it up. Don't deal with it! And again, the fear of pain really gets in the way.

But the enemy isn't the pain! (I know you will find this hard to believe.) The enemy is the *fear!*

Fear of Failure

Scott was the star of the basketball team—and I mean, *star*. He averaged thirty-nine points, four steals, and twelve rebounds a game. Even though he was only five eleven, he could slam dunk. And he usually did, three or four times a game.

One week before the state tournament, Scott sprained a finger. He could still play. But with his hand taped up, his outside shots were just a little off—enough to cut his scoring percentage from 70 to 40 percent.

Then came the first round of the tournament. Scott shot the ball as much as ever. For some strange reason, his damaged finger made him forget there were four other guys out on the floor. He never passed the ball—just shot for the basket.

SLABS OF CONCRETE

By the third quarter, with his team down by twelve points, Scott was pulled from the game. For the first time in his life, he spent a whole quarter on the bench. And his team (picked by everybody to make the finals) was eliminated in the first round.

Scott had all sorts of excuses for the loss. He blamed the other players, the coach, and the guy who had collided with him and sprained his finger in the first place. Scott couldn't face the fact that he had failed. Big Scott, star basketball player, blew it!

But what's so bad about that? Why is failure such a disaster that Scott had to avoid it at all costs—even deny it when it happened? Why do people fear failure like it is a deadly disease?

The answer is all around you. You live in a society where success—what you do—is everything!

Think about it. A guy asks a buddy, "Who is that girl over there?" What will he answer? "She's a cheerleader." "She's the president of the French club." "She's a brain."

When adults get into a conversation, one of the first questions that comes up is "What do you do?" And how many times have you been asked, "What do you plan to do with your life?"

Right now, in our society, what you do is a lot more important than who you are. The nobodies at school are the people who don't do anything other people see as valuable. They are not in a club, on the student council, on a team,

WHO'S GONNA LOVE ME?

or in a play. They can't be identified by their actions. So, they become *invisible*. They have no identity—no worth.

You can't measure somebody's spirit. Can you imagine overhearing this conversation?

"Who is that?"

"A person with a wonderful spirit—a real child of God."

"Wow, would I like to meet *him!*"

But since we have such a rough time measuring spirit, we settle for something we *can* measure—achievements! Successful people are good to know. People who fail are not! Simple as that. I am worth getting to know if I am successful. Who I am is measured by what I do—how I succeed.

Back in the time of Jesus, there was sort of an ultimate failure—the leper. Leprosy was a dreaded disease. Leprosy starts out as ulcers on the skin and slowly eats away at the body. After a while, lepers start losing fingers and toes, then whole limbs, until finally they die an ugly death. Back then, lepers walked around ringing little bells, making others aware of their disease. When they came near healthy people, the lepers had to cry out, "Unclean, unclean!" They were ugly outcasts in their society. (You can imagine the talk behind Jesus' back. You see, Jesus had this habit of *caring* about lepers.)

Today, failure is like a form of leprosy. If Scott allowed himself to fail on the basketball court, he thought no one would like him. He

SLABS OF CONCRETE

would be shunned like the nobodies. He would be a failure. He wouldn't need to ring a bell or cry out, "Failure, failure!" because everyone would know it. He would be an ugly outcast.

So Scott's fear of failure drove him to try to overachieve on the basketball court. His self-worth was based on how many points he could score each game. Each game in the win column made him feel better about himself. Each loss was a blow to his self-esteem.

With his self-worth on the line every game, Scott certainly couldn't trust his teammates to put points on the board. If they failed, it would reflect poorly on him. So he had to do it all himself.

And to admit failure on the court was the same as admitting failure in life for Scott. He believed that unless he achieved in basketball, he was no good. Better to blame everyone else than to admit defeat.

You probably know an overachiever or two. But a lot more people face the fear of failure in another way. They *refuse to try!* "I won't take clarinet because I might not be good at it." "I won't go out for the team because I probably won't make it." "I won't join the club because I probably can't keep the rules." And on and on and on!

Some of those in groups, or cliques, you looked at earlier succeed at failure. "If you can't succeed at success, then at least succeed at failing." So, some kids fail very, very well.

WHO'S GONNA LOVE ME?

They see how many classes they can skip, how many courses they can bungle up, how much property they can destroy. Then, they sit back and brag about their "battle stories." The big things are the last confrontation with the principal, the latest hassle with a police officer, a feud with parents. (Such a needless rebellion has only one hero!)

Other groups believe in the image of success at all costs. They lie, cheat, and steal to keep up the image of success. And anybody lucky enough to belong to the group is expected to do the same. If you belonged to a clique like this and decided you didn't want to cheat anymore, could you admit that to your friends?

Sometimes the only reason you can see for achieving in school in the first place is because your parents expect it. Or you *believe* they expect it. Your parents like you if you get A's and B's. They don't like you if you get C's and D's. (Get an F, and you will be locked in the cellar without food and water!)

When everybody around you is judging your worth by what you do, failure is a very, very scary thing. Sometimes the fear is so strong that you miss the joy of just being you.

A LITTLE SLAB OF CONCRETE

I used to hear people say, "The only thing we have to fear is fear itself." I would scratch my head and wonder what *that* could mean. I am beginning to understand the sentence. Fear sets up a vicious circle that traps a person in more and more fear.

Fear of rejection kept Kevin from asking Meg out. With the hint of rejection from his one feeble attempt, Kevin has now played out a real rejection hundreds of times in his mind. So, even though he never gave Meg the chance to reject him, he still feels rejected. And he acts rejected.

Because Debbie's dad feared pain, he ignored the pain Debbie was feeling. When pain is ignored, so is the cause of the pain, the injury. And since Debbie's dad didn't see the injury he caused, he will probably cause more injuries and more pain.

In a TV movie, a college running back injured his knee during the championship game. He went to the locker room where he got a shot in the knee. The whole area was numbed so he wouldn't feel the pain. He went back in the game. After another quarter, the knee was hit again, and again the trainers shot drugs into it. Finally, on a long run for the end zone, the player's knee collapsed. The team won the game, but this young man never played football again.

Emotional pain works the same way. I feel bad about myself because I'm not a good student. If I numb the pain with drugs, I become a worse student. And the downward spiral continues.

WHO'S GONNA LOVE ME?

If I confront and heal the injury—my poor self-esteem—I start feeling better about myself. And I start climbing out of my rut.

Because Scott feared failure, he focused all his time and energy in an area where he could succeed. And because he spent all his time on the basketball court, Scott failed in academics. Instead of facing his fear, Scott focused even more energy on basketball. His fear of failure caused his failure and (this is *really scary!*) causes him to fear failure even more. So, he is trapped, and the downward spiral continues.

All of these fears get their power from my insecurities:

- If I am rejected, it's my fault, not *theirs*. It's because I'm no good—it can't be because *they* don't see the goodness in me.
- If I feel pain, it's because there's something wrong with me. Heroes don't feel pain—they live happily ever after. Good people don't feel pain.
- If I fail, it means I'm no good. Only successful people are good.

Because I'm no good, I try to find my worth outside of myself. I am good because I belong to the popular clique. I am good because I listen to a certain type of music. I am good because I skipped class two times without getting caught.

SLABS OF CONCRETE

And now the stage is set for *turf wars*. I know what is good for me—my group. Don't try to change my mind. If you reject my group, I'll reject your group. You reject my group because it's rich—I reject your group because it's poor. My group is black—your group is white. My group likes soul music—your group likes heavy metal.

In cities, gangs who have nothing to defend are defending it with their lives. "I will shoot other people for our slab of twisted concrete. And I will die in order to protect it because the turf is good. The group is good—worth more than my life. And we are good because we belong to the group."

What's your slab of concrete? What are you defending with your soul? Your clothes? Your grades? Your drugs? Your music? Your life? And what is it costing you in the process?

"Whoa, Father Don!"

"This is supposed to be helping! Who are you trying to kid?"

"You make me want to run right out and try relationships!"

Well, from what I have said so far, conditional relationships do seem like a waste of time. But teen life is full of them. Why do people put up with these relationships?

Why do you?

3

Look in the Mirror

- Your message is so loud I can't hear you!
- Hey! People really are talking behind my back.
- I am only on the way to being me—so back off!
- What's love got to do with it, anyway? I have to know!

WHO'S GONNA LOVE ME?

Pretend for a minute that you just got a job herding sheep. (So, it isn't in your career plans. Play along with me for a minute.) Anyway, you want to keep your sheep contained in a certain area. You would fence them in, right? But what if you wanted them to move around—graze in different areas? Seems stupid to keep building fences and tearing them down. So what would you use?

How about *string?*

Right! Those sheep could break down, chew through, and trample over string in two seconds!

Well, some cagey scientists proved just the opposite. First of all, they set up a portable electric fence. Every time a sheep got too close? Zap! The poor creature got a little shock.

Pretty soon, the electric wire was replaced with a piece of string. The sheep didn't know the difference, so they stayed away from the string. Even the next generation of sheep shied away from the string. The sheep passed on to the lambs the message that the string was dangerous.

People often behave like sheep. Did you ever know people who were deathly afraid of dogs? These people probably have stories about a bad experience with a dog when they were young. And even though they know, in their minds, that not all dogs are mean, when they get around a dog, their feelings take over. And they are scared.

LOOK IN THE MIRROR

You are receiving messages all the time, both verbal messages and messages sent by experiences. You accept some of those messages and use them to build your images of the world, of other people, and of yourself.

One difference between your world and the world your parents grew up in is the number of messages you receive. You are right in the middle of the biggest information explosion in history. That means you get hit with and have access to more information than any other people before you—ever!

So what are some of the messages you get hit with? Let's look at the news first.

- Four or five years ago, you couldn't turn on the television without seeing somebody starving in Ethiopia. The message got out that there were people in the world who did not have enough to eat. Some celebrities got together to help solve the problem, and there was Band Aid, USA for Africa, and Live Aid. (Don't forget Farm Aid, Comic Relief, and Hands across America.) All that made hunger (and poverty and homelessness) big news. Today, that is old news. There are just as many hungry, poor, and homeless people, but the message is gone from the air.
- Then an important television evangelist got involved in a sex scandal. That made

WHO'S GONNA LOVE ME?

for pretty juicy news throughout North America. So the message got out that television evangelists are not what they seem to be. All preachers suffered—their ministries lost millions of dollars in contributions.
- Political candidates make for big news, too. But sometimes it is hard to find out what a candidate stands for. One married guy who was running for president of the United States got involved with another woman (maybe you remember). Well, all people wanted to talk about was the sex and the scandal. His race for the White House was over.

Messages in the news give you images of the world—what kind of place it is, what people are like, what is important. These messages can be very, very loud. They can even drown out your own thoughts about things.

Your parents also send you messages about the world. Are your parents liberal, conservative, or independent? Do they save their money? Or do they spend, spend, spend? Do they enjoy meaningful careers? Are they stuck in jobs they hate? Like it or not, your world has been shaped by your parents.

Kath's mother grew up just outside Newark, New Jersey. She saw the city go downhill (as big cities sometimes do). There were many reasons

LOOK IN THE MIRROR

why Newark was no longer the garden spot of the Garden State. Kath's mother was convinced that the fall of Newark was caused by the coming of the blacks. The riots of the mid-1960s helped to convince her even more.

Now Kath got this message from her mom in many ways over the years. Kath's sister came home from school one day with a black guy. Mom had a fit! She would not allow the girl ever to see him again. Once on a vacation, the family drove through a black neighborhood in Philadelphia. Kath's mom had another fit—made the family lock all the car doors. She started saying prayers and didn't stop until they were out of the city.

When she was little, Kath just took this message for granted. As she grew older, she started to question the message—even confronted her mother one day. But nothing changed. The attitude was too ingrained. Kath continues to hear messages about fearing blacks.

That doesn't mean that Kath has to accept her mother's images and make them her own. Kath may or may not choose to be as prejudiced as her mother. That's not the point. All around you are these loud messages. Some may be good. Some are bad. But with all these messages, it is very hard for you to hear the truth. It is easy to chase after the images in the messages.

Moses had a little image problem with the Israelites. The Israelites had lived a long time in Egypt. They had been soaking up the messages of Egyptian culture. Oh sure, they were slaves, but they did look up to the Egyptians. And the Egyptians seemed to have all these idols—little statues that were supposed to have a lot of power.

Well, God picked Moses to lead the Israelites out of slavery in Egypt. Moses pointed out that God was not a statue! God was a person. The people went along with this. (They were getting out of slavery, after all.)

But then came Moses' big visit to Mount Sinai. Moses went up to the mountain. He was supposed to be getting this covenant with God. But he was gone a very, very long time.

Moses had left his brother Aaron in charge. So, the people went to Aaron. "Aaron, build us one of those gods to be our leader! Moses may never come back." Aaron was between a rock and a hard place. But he let the people have their way. Because their image of god was a fancy statue, they built themselves a golden calf and started worshiping it.

All the messages the Israelites had received about God affected their images. They accepted Moses' image for a while. Then they tossed it.

Oh, by the way, when Moses got back from Mount Sinai, he was *really* ticked. He gave the Israelites an earful—and they did turn back to the true God. (So much for golden calves.)

You get messages all the time. Sometimes it is a lot easier for you to build yourself a little golden calf—to settle for the easy images—than it is to seek out the truth. Your images of your friends, family, school, even your image of yourself need to be challenged. Then you can accept the images, reject them, or change them.

RUMORS CAN KILL YOU

Did you ever start a rumor! Fun, isn't it? All you have to do is hint at something, and before you know it, the message is coming back at you. "Jill thinks there will be a geometry quiz tomorrow" comes back in an hour as "There is going to be a big geometry test tomorrow, and it is going to count as half the grade!"

A lot of the messages you hear are really rumors. Our friend Kim suffered from rumors. When the band members heard the rumor that she was a burnout, they took that message and processed it with the images they had of Kim. They folded in their images of the senders of the message. They stacked it up with the images of their clique. They then made the decision to accept this new message about Kim. Bang! That quick, Kim was rejected. (The group's own fear of rejection and need to belong helped the process.)

Oh, maybe a few brave souls stood up for Kim. But they were pushed out to the fringe of the clique. They also fell from the good graces of the leaders. Some others probably didn't believe the rumors, but they were too scared to say anything.

Once a message is out, the truth of the message may not even matter. It's the image the receivers end up with, and what they do based on the message, that matters. That is the power of rumors.

You've probably known somebody who has been deeply affected by rumors. An old woman lives alone in a big old house. Some kids spread the rumor around the neighborhood that she's a witch. She is obviously not a witch, but kids stay away from her anyway. Maybe even some adults start to mistrust her. She is left alone and bewildered.

A guy in high school loves his ballet lessons. He has real talent and wants to dance professionally. Some kids start talking about his sexual preference. All of a sudden people start treating him as if he is gay!

Your chemistry teacher hears from your last year's biology teacher that you cheat on exams. Even though it may not be true, your chemistry teacher has an image of you as a cheater and watches you like a hawk.

That's the negative side of rumors about others. Rumors can have a positive side. If a new girl comes to school, and word gets around that she is a great person to know, people will go out of their way to meet her. If the junior varsity coach drops the word that you are a great player, you will have a lot easier time making the varsity (even if you don't do all that well at tryouts). But let's face it, most people do not spread rumors about how wonderful you are.

What Are They Saying about You?

Not only do you receive messages about the world and others, you also receive messages about yourself. Do you remember those TV spots that warned parents to listen to what their children were hearing from them?

"Hey, stupid! Don't you ever listen?"
"Can't you do anything right?"
"You're pathetic."
"I wish you were never born."

The parents in the spot are sending some pretty negative messages to their kids. Those messages hurt. But it is possible to get some positive messages, too.

"I like you."
"You've got a good sense of humor."
"You're a good listener."
"I appreciate your openness and honesty."

The words of others reveal their images of you. So do their actions. When someone hugs you, that action says you are worth hugging. When someone ignores you, that action says you are not worth paying attention to.

A divorce sends lots of messages to children. The messages may not be what the parents mean to say to their children. For example, the parents may know that they are responsible for

WHO'S GONNA LOVE ME?

the divorce. But a child doesn't see it that way. He or she may think, "This must be my fault! I must be a bad kid! If I had done my chores and eaten my oatmeal, this would never have happened!"

You don't even have to know somebody to let them give you images of yourself. When the woman coos over the television screen that you will smell great if you buy this new perfume, she is letting you think that you smell pretty awful right now.

You listen to a lot of music, don't you? Well, almost all radio stations air up to eighteen minutes of commercials every hour. And your ears are right there! That means for eighteen minutes out of sixty, somebody is telling you what you need to be a better you. Way underneath all that is a very loud message—you are *not* okay the way you are.

Hey, if all the messages you got about yourself were accurate, you would have a pretty clear picture about yourself. But (rumor has it) not all these messages are accurate—some are downright distorted.

- Every time Carol's mother looks at Carol, she is reminded of her ex-husband. As much as the mother tries not to, sometimes she treats Carol as if Carol were the man whom she now despises. Carol receives the message that she is disliked, even hated.

LOOK IN THE MIRROR

- Mrs. Carson has been a teacher for seventeen years. She is convinced that 90 percent of all students cheat. So, instead of praising Mary for her steadily improving performance, Mrs. Carson warns her about the consequences if she is caught cheating. Mary realizes that Mrs. Carson sees her as a cheater.
- Jim is a six five, 250-pound lineman—and all 250 pounds is muscle. When the freshmen in school see him coming, they move out of the way. Jim gets the message that he is awesome.

With all these messages coming in, which ones do you believe about yourself? It's not just the messages that are sent, it's how you believe them. The messages that you believe about yourself will make up your *self-image*. Then new messages are compared to that self-image. You either accept them and adjust your self-image, or you reject them if they don't agree closely enough with what you already believe. The messages you receive and believe become your mirror. And sometimes what you see in the mirror is just not that clear!

SELF-IMAGE

Where do self-images come from, anyway? It seems that the way you arrive at an image of

WHO'S GONNA LOVE ME?

yourself is a complicated matter. Even the experts aren't quite sure how it all happens. Most agree that you were born with some seed of a self-image, and your environment—including parents, friends, society, circumstances, and so on—helps you build the rest. People have been arguing about how much is inborn and how much is learned for thousands of years. (So, I am not going to try to solve it here.)

No one is completely sure when you start to believe what you believe about yourself. But most agree that by your teenage years, your self-image is pretty well formed—good or bad. There are certain messages you believe, and certain messages you don't believe.

When Matt was eighteen months old, his sister was born with a severe handicap. Matt's parents tried their best to give Matt equal time, but he received some very clear messages: "You are loved when you're nice to your sister. You are loved when you stay out of the way and are well behaved. You are loved only when you're good enough." So, Matt built his self-image around good behavior.

Because of this self-image, Matt focuses all of his energy on achievement. He's a fastidious student, a "neat freak," an impeccable dresser. He's a soloist in the band, captain of the soccer team, and vice-president of the student council.

Matt craves praise since he believes his goodness comes from his accomplishments. And so he surrounds himself with people who appre-

LOOK IN THE MIRROR

ciate his efforts. His friends tend to be less accomplished than Matt—the kind who will be impressed with his achievements.

Success is worth any cost to Matt. He and his friends play the game well. They're the teacher's pets, the kids who nobody believes would cheat on an exam. Matt loves to be called an "outstanding young man."

Deep down, though, Matt never feels *really* outstanding. He never feels good enough. He'll never score enough goals, get enough top grades, or get enough praise. Matt is convinced that even God doesn't love him. God can see all the games Matt is playing and knows that he isn't really being all that good. (Poor Matt!)

But Matt is hooked! He has to keep up the front, even if it is based on nothing! Matt is hooked on the praise of teachers, parents, friends, everybody. So, Matt has to keep coming up with achievements—to keep the praise rolling in.

Matt has a negative self-image. His fear of failure is extreme. It affects everything he does, even his choice of friends. Matt is a praise addict because he believes that he is worth something only when he is receiving that praise.

What a trap! All Matt's choices reinforce his image of himself. The more praise he receives, the worse things get.

Maybe you know somebody like Matt. Or maybe you know someone that's hooked on knowledge. ("I am loved only for my intelligence.") Somebody hooked on appearance. ("I am loved only because I'm cute.") Somebody hooked on status. ("I am loved because I am the president of the club.")

What's Your Message about You?

What does your self-image look like? You can get a good picture of your self-image by looking in the message mirror. What messages do you believe about yourself? First, figure out the negative messages you believe about yourself. That's not all that hard to do. Just listen to your wish list:

- "I wish I were as pretty as Shannon." (Self-image: "I'm ugly.")
- "I wish some girls would notice me." (Self-image: "I'm not 'man' enough to be noticed.")
- "I wish I could stand up to that bully." (Self-image: "I'm a chicken.")
- "I wish I were more popular." (Self-image: "I'm not likable.")

Wishes usually reveal some real negative stuff about your self-image.

Now, if you are interested in some more positive messages, look at what you *really* like to do. (Skip the stuff you are supposed to like. Concentrate on the truth here.)

LOOK IN THE MIRROR

- "I love to play sports." (Self-image: "I consider myself coordinated and athletic—at the very least, eager.")
- "I love to listen to my friends' problems." (Self-image: "I consider myself helpful and sympathetic.")
- "I love to write poetry." (Self-image: "I consider myself sensitive and good with words.")

You get the idea. Why don't you stick your thumb in this book for a couple minutes. Stare at the ceiling (or the clouds) and see if you can't come up with a wish list and a "love-to-do" list.

Welcome back! Which was harder—the wishes or the good stuff? If you are normal, it is a lot easier to think about the negative messages about yourself than it is to think about the positive ones. Positive self-images can be hard to come by. Anyhow, as you make up these lists in your head, you are getting a fairly good idea of what *you* think about *you!*

If you have a longer list of wishes, you probably have a negative self-image. If you have a longer list of the good stuff, yours is pretty positive. This basic self-image has a big impact on your view of others, the world, and God. People with negative self-images believe that they are unlovable or that they have to *earn* love. People with positive self-images believe that they are lovable for who they are and not for what they do.

WHO'S GONNA LOVE ME?

If you have a negative self-image, you could be doing some destructive things to yourself. People with eating disorders, drug or alcohol problems, or really bad tempers almost always have extremely poor self-images. This doesn't mean they *are* bad, but they *see themselves* as bad. Other people with poor self-images may get hooked on compulsive shopping or compulsive gambling. They may become workaholics, or they may become very dependent on other people to take care of them or do their thinking for them. People with poor self-images can get sucked into cults, too, because cult leaders really make hay with poor self-images.

Your self-image affects your images of others, too. If you believe you're basically good, you probably believe that other people are basically good. If you believe you're basically bad, you may believe that others are the same way.

If you are a perfectionist, you may expect the same of others. And your friends always seem to disappoint you because they aren't perfect. If you believe your self-worth comes from your good deeds, you'll always be trying to please others. You start to look at everybody as a potential customer for your services.

Your self-image and your image of others together affect your image of the world. If all people are basically good, the world is an exciting place to be in. If all people are basically bad, then the world is rotten, and you need a place to hide!

LOOK IN THE MIRROR

Throughout your life, you have also received many messages about God, and the images you accept are a reflection of your self-image. (That is a dirty trick to play on God. You were made in God's image, and here you are trying to make God in your image.)

If you believe you are basically good, your images of God will probably include father, mother, friend, confidant, and so on. If you believe you are basically bad, you may have images of God as cop, judge, master, boss, and so on.

SO, WHERE IS THE LOVE?

Why do you put up with conditional relationships? The answer to that question lies in your self-image.

Remember Jenny? She believes that sex is the way to hold on to Todd. She believes that because everyone around her has sent her that message. She has chosen to accept that message and make it part of her self-image. Even if she heard the message that it is okay *not* to have sex with somebody she was going with, she missed it (or chose to ignore it). In her world, that is the way things are!

But Jenny has accepted the message that sex has to be a part of her relationship with Todd because she doesn't believe in herself. She can't believe that Todd could love her just for herself. He loves her for the sexual pleasure she

WHO'S GONNA LOVE ME?

gives him, for her status as a cheerleader, maybe even for her help with math—but never for just being Jenny.

Admit it! You want to be loved. Everybody does. Remember, "It is *not good* to be alone." But all those conditions and messages (and negative self-images) can get in the way of love. As long as you are stuck in conditional relationships and are surrounded by bad images, what you see when you look in the mirror is pretty dark. You don't look very lovable.

So you climb into another group, accept the conditions, act the way the group wants you to act, dress the way the group wants you to dress. And you accept everything as the price you pay to belong. You are left with that negative self-image.

What if there was a way to brighten up that image in the mirror? What if there was another way of relating? What if (out there—right now) there was some love that had *no* strings? Well, there is!

Conditional acceptance is a dead-end street, not a pathway to love. So, you are going to have to start kicking down the conditional relationships. If you are looking for love, conditions are in the way. Every condition put on behavior is a roadblock on the way to the point of true love.

Of course, you are going to have to start fighting the fears, too. What you are going to have to do is start risking rejection, pain, and

LOOK IN THE MIRROR

failure. (If you thought I was going to make this easy, you were wrong.)

God Gets into the Act

Unconditional love—love without strings—was God's idea. ("Father Don has to say that. It's what he does. He's a professional at the God stuff!") I would like to tell you that I made that up, but I didn't.

Look, you want real love. You want to know where to find this unconditional love. Well, you find it in the same place you find the big *ifs*—in relationships (but definitely not in the same kinds of relationships). This is where God comes in. Not only is unconditional love God's idea, God shows up in those relationships.

You *can* find God in good relationships. And you can have a good relationship with God. But you are going to have to get rid of some of the old images of God as a mean old judge—just waiting for you to slip so that punishment can come crashing down on your head! Your relationship with God can be like your relationship with your best friend.

This may blow some of your images of God. But God loves you, cares for you, guides you, and challenges you. Jesus even called God "Abba." That word doesn't mean "Father"—it means "Dad"!

Your own parents may not have been all that wonderful. So, calling God "Father" may

WHO'S GONNA LOVE ME?

not get the point across all that well. If your father left you and your mom, you might push that image on God. If your mother has a drinking problem, looking at God in the parent image might be tough. But when people started calling God "Father," it was their way of jerking God out of the heavens and locating all that powerful divinity smack dab in human relationships. God isn't *out there.* God is *right here!*

There are a lot of "God" images floating around. Maybe you think of God as a force. Maybe you look at God as creator. Some God images are cold, distant, judgmental. The Bible (God's Book) becomes just a big rule book—a book filled with so many traps that you can almost never make it through a day without sinning. So, life becomes a big obstacle course. You have to run fast and dodge hard, or you will be zapped by God.

Now I am going to challenge all those images of God. They are just people's self-images that have run wild. God is love. God is personal. You can treat God as a friend (and that is the way God is going to treat you).

You can talk to God, too. You can start to look at the Bible as a book of helpful stories handed over to you by a good friend. You might even start wanting to spend some time with this friend. You might even grow in your love for this friend.

Now, if you want to keep your image of God as a big bully who is putting more and more

LOOK IN THE MIRROR

conditions and demands on you, I can't stop you. In reality, God is not too interested in putting demands on you. God is about handling the demands that are already there. God is about getting rid of burdens, not taking on a new load of them.

God already loves you *unconditionally.* God does not put strings on you. If you really want to break out of the conditional trap, you are going to have to start looking at life in a new way. You are going to have to challenge your own images of God, friendship, love—and your self-image, too.

What you will discover is not easy, but it is *great!*

4

Love Without Strings

■

- Does anybody know the way out of this mess?
- Trust me! This is the way I am—take it or leave it!
- You're trying to tell me love is where the action is?
- Can anything last forever?
- Still, there has to be something in this for me!

WHO'S GONNA LOVE ME?

I am going to tell you a story. Really it is kind of a fable—maybe even a fairy tale. Don't get too hung up on the kind of story it is. (Of course, there will be a good moral at the end of the story. Why would I tell it otherwise?)

Here goes. In a fancy kingdom, there lived two fair maidens—Priscilla and Penelope. They were the twin daughters of the king. The king had no other children. Because he was very old and knew he would die soon, he called upon his two daughters.

"I am old and will die soon," he told them, "and one of you will wear my crown." The daughters were mighty competitive. Right away they started arguing about who should be the next ruler.

"Oh, shut up!" shouted the old king. "My fair daughters, I cannot choose between you. Instead, I think I'll send you on a little quest." (You may have noticed that quests are pretty common in this kind of story.)

"In a place not far from here," continued the king, "there flows some fine, sweet water that wells up from the Spring of Forever. Only a few brave souls have ever found this place. I have never tasted this water myself." The king paused to think about the wonderful taste this water must have. "To get to the point, the first one of you to bring me a cup of the water from the Spring of Forever will be the next ruler!"

This sounded like a pretty stupid way to pick a ruler. But the girls knew that once the old

LOVE WITHOUT STRINGS

man made up his mind, nothing was going to change it. So the maidens hopped right to it. Each was confident that she would find the spring before her sister did.

Priscilla ran straight into the forest. She was sure the spring would be flowing from a magical knoll she had heard about. She was no more than a few hundred yards into the forest when she bumped into a young forester named Hilman. He was felling a tree. (Ever notice that in these stories people *fell* trees? In real life, people *chop trees down!*)

"Excuse me," barked Priscilla, interrupting the swing of Hilman's ax. She looked around to make sure no one was listening. Then she said, "I am looking for the Spring of Forever."

"Never heard of it," snapped Hilman. He mopped his brow with an old rag and pulled a flask from his hip pocket. "This is the best water I've ever tasted," he said. And he shoved the flask under Priscilla's nose.

The smell made Priscilla's nose wrinkle. She took a sip and spit it out. "Bleah," she snorted. "This tastes like rust! It is bitter." She spit about five times, trying to get the taste out of her mouth.

"Listen, young lady," Hilman said, jabbing his finger at the girl. "I've worked in these forests all my life. Water doesn't get any better than this."

"Oh, but it has to," said Priscilla. And she told Hilman all about her quest, her father, his old age, her chance to be the next ruler. She told him that the Spring of Forever had this fine, sweet water that wells up from who knows where. And she finished with her own hunch about the magical knoll.

"I have a live one here!" thought Hilman. "She is a real princess and she may become queen. If I help her find the Spring of Forever, she will be forever indebted to me." Hilman knew a good thing when it bumped into him, so he volunteered to help Priscilla find the spring.

Meanwhile, back in the kingdom, Penelope had decided to hang around the village for a while. Her father had said that a few brave souls had found the spring before. So, she thought she might be able to dig up one of them. She asked the villagers who they thought was the bravest person in the land. Nine out of ten of them directed her to a guy named Keepsa.

Keepsa lived on the edge of the village in a ramshackled old hut. He was a very, *very* old man. But when Penelope asked him about the Spring of Forever, his eyes twinkled like a kid's at Christmas.

"Your father is a wise king," Keepsa told Penelope, "and you were wise to come to me."

"Then you know where the Spring of Forever wells up?" Penelope was *so* excited.

"Each person must find her own path to the place where the Spring of Forever rises," said the old man—his voice loaded with mystery. (Lines like that give fairy tales a bad name.)

LOVE WITHOUT STRINGS

"But I can help you find your path." Off they went—out of the village and up into the green pastureland.

By this time, Priscilla and Hilman were deep in the forest. They were not doing too well. They stopped at every brook, every stream, every puddle. Looking for new sources of water, they tapped every rock. But all the water they tasted was worse than the water in Hilman's flask.

Priscilla was getting used to Hilman's bitter water. The longer they walked, the thirstier she got. The thirstier she got, the more of Hilman's water she drank.

Finally, Priscilla and Hilman came to a clearing in the woods. Nothing much—just a simple clearing. (Hardly a magical knoll.) But her eyes were tired and the light was dim. A small, deep pond stood in the center of the clearing. "This must be it!" sang Priscilla. She cupped the pond water in her hands.

The water was cloudy, but Priscilla failed to notice. It had a strange odor, but it sure smelled better than the rusty stuff she had been drinking. And the taste—well, it was not as bitter as Hilman's water.

Priscilla brushed the hair out of her eyes. "Do you suppose this is it?" she asked Hilman as he bent over to sample it himself.

"Must be!" said Hilman confidently. "Best water I've ever tasted." Hilman dumped out his own flask and refilled it with water from the pond. The two weary travelers began their trek to the castle.

Back in the pastureland, Penelope also ran to every brook and stream she saw. But at each one Keepsa would say, "This is fine water. It is clear and crisp and sweet. But there is better water still."

And every time, Penelope would say, "Better than this? But this water is so good!"

Finally, they came to an abandoned water trough—where horses used to drink. "There!" cried Keepsa. "There is the water from the Spring of Forever."

Penelope was *so* surprised. Who could've guessed the place where the fine, sweet water welled forth would be so ordinary? But when she tasted the water in the trough, she knew Keepsa was right. She filled a cup with the water, and the two journeyed back to the castle.

By the time Penelope and Keepsa got to the castle, Priscilla had thrown her water (and Hilman) out the window. When she poured the water from the flask into a cup, she saw how yucky it looked. The water was no darn good. It even tasted worse than common castle water.

LOOKING FOR A GUIDE?

If this were a real fairy tale, I'd have Penelope come rushing in to claim the crown. Keepsa would drink the water and be zapped into a

LOVE WITHOUT STRINGS

handsome prince. (He might even become prime minister.) Of course, the two would marry and live happily ever after.

But let's skip all that and get right to the moral of the story. What was the difference between the two sisters? It wasn't so much that the sisters were different. Their guides were different.

Hilman, at his young age, thought that he had experienced the best that life had to offer. He had settled for whatever he stumbled upon, and he convinced Priscilla to do the same.

When Priscilla started out, she had a grand vision of what she was looking for. But after a while, her experiences with the bitter water changed her perception. What she finally thought was fine, sweet water was in fact not much better than the stuff she had spit out in the beginning.

Meanwhile, Penelope found a wise old guide, one who she believed had tasted the fine, sweet water of the Spring of Forever. Keepsa knew what Penelope was looking for, even more than she did.

So the secret to finding the place where the fine, sweet water welled up from the Spring of Forever was in finding someone who had been there and in asking for this person's guidance.

Guess what! That's the secret to finding unconditional love. I can't give you a complete definition of unconditional love. I can't tell you exactly what it looks like or where to find it (for sure). But I'll bet you've caught glimpses of it in some of your relationships.

You don't need to find the bravest person in the village to start your journey toward unconditional love. Your path to love will be a little different from anyone else's.

You can't even get there by reading what I have to say about unconditional love. Suppose you had never seen the mountains. I can show you photographs of them, and I can tell you what an incredible experience it is to hike in them. But until you experience the mountains yourself, you won't know exactly what I'm talking about. Yup, the photographs are beautiful. You may even get excited by my excitement. But it's still not the same.

You can know all *about* something. You can read about it, think about it, hear about it, see movies about it. But until you've experienced it yourself, it's only head knowledge. You don't really *know* something until you've experienced it.

So I'm going to guide you a little bit. I am going to tell you *about* unconditional love. We'll journey through a few experiences of it. I'll even point out some of its principles and benefits. You may recognize some of your own experiences in the stories I tell. Seek out the people in those experiences. They might be the ones to lead you to your own Spring of Forever.

You might have to rethink some of your ideas of love. I hope you have some better ways to do your rethinking after you read this chapter. Maybe, very soon, you will bump into some unconditional love. You'll remember this chapter and say, "Ha! That's what Father Don was talking about!"

Enough chatter. Let's go to the mountains.

I AM A PERSON

When I was in my junior year of high school, I had a teacher who was obviously amused by my classroom antics. I was a real show-off in school, and I found myself showing off for her. She would giggle and laugh, and then she'd have to get control of the class and calm down. After a while I was just clowning around to get her attention. I wanted her to notice me.

Then one day, she stopped me in the hallway. She stared right at me and said, "I'm enjoying you, but you don't have to play games to get my attention. I'll give it to you."

I tried to be cool about it. "What d'ya mean?" I asked, even though I knew she had my number.

"You're worth paying attention to. You're an interesting person. And I hope you'll give me a chance to help explore that with you."

Now how do you respond to something like that? No one ever tells you how to respond. So I tried to crack another joke, or trip and fall, instead of really responding. But after that, I no-

WHO'S GONNA LOVE ME?

ticed that I didn't goof off as much in class. I didn't need to. The game was over. She had called it. And I wanted it to be over.

I can't tell you too much of what I learned in that teacher's class. I can tell you that she showed me *unconditional love*. She didn't approve of my behavior. She *saw through* my behavior and realized that I needed to be recognized and noticed by her—as a person. That little story gives you a very important principle of this love without strings.

> *Principle 1*
> *Love without strings accepts the person, but not necessarily the behavior.*

This principle doesn't mean that people who love you unconditionally have to reject your behavior all the time. It just means that when you mess up, they still accept you.

That's a little different than the way the band kids treated Kim. She was accepted *until* she messed up (not in spite of the fact that she messed up). Love without strings is unconditional—it has no *ifs* attached to it. I love you. Period.

Do You Really Love Me?

When I was in high school, I also played wingback and safety for the football team. I was one

LOVE WITHOUT STRINGS

of the smallest players. I didn't have all the physical skills that the big kids had. At first I tried running over the big guys. But after picking helmet fragments out of my teeth, I found I needed a better way to play.

I didn't always do everything right, and my coach would yell and scream at me just as he did with everybody else. But what I could do, I did.

I used speed to go around the big guys. I used my head. What I lacked in physical talent, I made up for in effort. And my coach *noticed!* He stopped one day and told me that I had found the right way to play the game.

My coach didn't encourage me for my size or my strength. He didn't support me because I was one of his best players. Instead he encouraged *me!* He noticed my determination. He encouraged my spirit. He supported Don Kimball—the person. He was not just interested in my performance.

> *Principle 2*
> *Love without strings affirms personhood—not necessarily achievements.*

This is close to Principle 1, but it has a different twist. In addition to not being judged by my negative behavior, I also am not judged by my success. Ever get the feeling people like you just because of what you do for *them?* ("You make me feel so fine!") That is not unconditional love.

Everybody needs affirmation. Affirmation is the simple act of noticing and communicating positive things about *who* a person is. Affirmation goes after *qualities,* not accomplishments. You get personal affirmation when somebody encourages your determination, perseverance, sense of humor, patience, enthusiasm, courage, and spirit. Affirmation can't be earned. It is something people do for you when they love you.

My high school coach was quite a guy! He would have affirmed me even if I were the designated bench warmer. He appreciated my presence on the team as much as he appreciated the star quarterback. Hey, he loved me!

Love Does!

Karen felt affirmation from her friend Carolyn. Karen was the class brain, solo clarinetist, starting goalie for the soccer team, and a leader in the youth group at church. (I know. You wish you had some of those problems yourself. But remember, success isn't everything.)

Karen was never sure if people liked her for herself, or because of her accomplishments—or worse, what they could get from her. But Carolyn seemed to have no investment in Karen. They weren't in the same classes. Carolyn wasn't too interested in sports or the clarinet.

LOVE WITHOUT STRINGS

During their free period, the two of them would go for long walks and just talk about life. They shared their concerns, embarrassing moments, and unanswered questions. They could laugh, cry, and have fun together.

A year after Karen went off to college, her family moved away from her hometown. Just a couple months later, Karen's dad was killed in a freak hotel fire. The day Karen arrived home for the funeral, there was a telegram from Carolyn waiting for her. "SORRY TO HEAR ABOUT YOUR DAD—STOP—I WILL BE THERE TOMORROW—STOP—LOVE CAROLYN!"

Carolyn drove four hundred miles to be with Karen and was there when Karen needed her most. Carolyn's love for Karen wasn't just a few shared words during free period. It was action.

> *Principle 3*
> *Love is a decision.*

You can't tell people you love them, and then not really love them. Nobody says, "I'll kiss you," and not kiss. The words *I love you* demand action. If the actions don't follow the words, the words are a lie.

Carolyn's love for Karen was expressed in her presence at the funeral. But it was also expressed in time spent together at school. It is still expressed in letters, phone conversations, visits, and a hundred other little ways. Carolyn has *decided* to love Karen. She means it.

The Ways of Love

That's how love is expressed between good friends. Parents show their love for their children not by just saying the words. They show it by being there for their children—with guidance, support, and even setting limits. (I want to go into limits later.)

Husbands and wives show their love for each other through some of the same actions that good friends share. They also express it through physical intimacy, lifelong commitment, and shared responsibility. (Brothers and sisters have ways of expressing their love for one another, too—I just can't seem to remember any of them right now.)

Even strangers can show real love. You have heard stories about people who risk their own lives for someone they have never met. I still get chills when I think of that news photo of the man helping people out of the frozen river after a plane crash. He helped several people get to safety. He never made it himself.

> *Principle 4*
> *Love without strings has many*
> *different expressions.*

LOVE WITHOUT STRINGS

One area that is confusing for everybody—especially teenagers—is romantic love. Your feelings tell you that this is love, but adults just smile and call it "puppy love." What's the difference? What's the difference between attraction and love without strings?

The problem, once again, is that no one can definitively tell you what's love and what's "just hormones." The first time you feel strong romantic attraction toward someone, it can be pretty heavy stuff. It's easy to say, "This *must* be love. I feel giddy every time I think of her or him. My stomach feels as if I'm about to go down a huge hill on a roller coaster. I get this goofy smile on my face."

Those are all feelings that go along with "falling in love." But they won't necessarily lead to a long-term love relationship. The only way you'll know if they will is time. (Don't hate me—I didn't make this up either!) I know, I know, you want to know *now* if this is love.

Look at all the principles of love I've mentioned so far. How do you know if people are loving you? Maybe they're just waiting until you've had enough time together to make mistakes. Maybe they're loving the help you give them with homework. If love is a decision, how can you know it's love until you've both had time to show it through your *actions?* Sorry, but it all boils down to time.

I'm not saying your relationship isn't the *beginning* of a long-term love relationship. You

WHO'S GONNA LOVE ME?

may very well stay with this person a long time, and maybe even marry him or her. The trick is keeping your expressions of love in line with the time-tested depth of your love.

Getting really physical when you first feel those love feelings is like giving someone a diamond ring because they said hello to you in the hall at school. Sexual intimacy in a relationship that's just starting out makes it that much more difficult to figure out if real love is present. Sex can be a pretty *if!*

You need to learn exactly which expressions of love go with which levels of love. And sexual intercourse is an expression of a lifetime commitment to another person. It simply is not appropriate outside the permanent commitment of marriage.

To look at it another way, sexual intercourse cannot be used to put strings on love. It is a celebration of lifelong, exclusive, committed love.

If you are not using sexual intercourse to express lifelong, committed love, what are you using it for? To feel more secure in the relationship? To prove your love? To show your friends how serious the relationship is? Or worse yet, to brag to your friends of another accomplishment? More strings, more conditions, more *ifs*.

Affection is a very important part of loving. Nobody was ever killed by a hug. But you might want to ask yourself why you want to hug somebody—for his or her sake, *or for yours!*

LOVE WITHOUT STRINGS

(Hey, it takes some living to get this all straight.) You are not going to be perfect in unconditional love all at once. But if you *want* love without strings, you have to *give* love without strings, too.

Love is not conditional or unconditional just because of the way you express it. But the appropriate expression of love between people depends on their roles and their relationships to one another. So, you may not kiss the school bus driver, but a kiss for your dad might be just right. You may hug a friend when you greet him or her, but you might get some stares if you hug the sales clerk after he wraps your package. (A little common sense can go a *long* way.)

There is a phrase people often use in love relationships (especially when they are fighting)—"I don't have to prove my love to you." Well, you do, and you don't. If by proving your love you mean having to express it sexually, well, no. You don't have to help your friend cheat on a test either.

But if you mean that your love doesn't have to go through any trials, guess again! When a friend shares confidences with you, you need to keep those confidences—not to *prove* your love, but to *act* on your love. When you hurt your friend, you need to seek forgiveness. The only proof anybody needs of somebody's love is love in action—doing loving things.

If your girlfriend says she loves you and then spends the whole week flirting with other guys (knowing how much that hurts you), she has proved, without a doubt, that she *does not* love you. The *ways* she shows her love have to match her *words* of love. Anytime somebody asks you to believe the words and ignore the actions, something isn't right.

Forever and for Always

Okay, one last story for one last principle in this chapter. As I said at the beginning, though, I'm telling you *about* unconditional love. These principles help you identify it, but they don't completely define it.

During his junior year, Eric got a new guidance counselor. The counselor called him down to her office one day, and he figured he was in some kind of trouble. After all, guidance counselors see you once a year in order to make up a schedule for the next year. The only other time they see you is when you're in trouble.

Mrs. Gentry was different. She had called Eric down just to meet him. She said she wanted to meet all the juniors because she knew they were facing some big decisions about college or careers.

She was easy to talk to. She knew about Eric's brother in twelfth grade and wanted to hear about their relationship. She knew about the trouble he had with the biology teacher the year before, and she seemed sincerely interested in Eric's side of the story. She seemed really in-

LOVE WITHOUT STRINGS

terested in Eric. Before the meeting was over, they set up another appointment just to talk some more.

They met several times in the coming months. Eric was cautious about opening up to Mrs. Gentry, but he also desperately wanted her acceptance. He told her about the problems in biology. Then he told her about his problems at home. Then he told her about his experimentation with drugs. At each turn, he expected her to reject him, to judge him, or to stop seeing him. But she didn't.

Finally, Eric told her about his suicide attempt. It had been such a feeble attempt that no one knew about it, and he couldn't believe he was sharing this with another human being. It was embarrassing, stupid, and very painful to talk about. She understood all that. She still accepted him, and she admired his strength in working through such a difficult time in his life.

Eric continued to see Mrs. Gentry regularly. He was in her office at least twice a week, if for no other reason than just to say hello.

After a few months, some of the other guidance counselors began to criticize Mrs. Gentry. They said she was spending too much time with Eric and a few other students. They gossiped about it. And one counselor even reported her to the principal. But Mrs. Gentry knew she had done nothing wrong. She let it be known that she would prefer to be fired than to tell her students to stop seeing her.

WHO'S GONNA LOVE ME?

Mrs. Gentry loved Eric. He tested her, and tested her, and tested her. He fully expected her to reject him at each turn. She didn't. She loved him enough even to risk her own job.

> *Principle 5*
> *Unconditional love lasts forever, no matter what.*

When people say "forever" and "no matter what," a lot of times they really mean "for now" or "if it feels good" or "if it doesn't cost me anything." So when people say or show you that they love you, you will probably throw tests at them.

"I love you."

"But did you know that I'm a lousy student?"

"Yes, but I still love you."

"Okay. But you know, I smoke and drink."

"Well, I don't like the smoking and drinking, but I still love you."

"What if I'm gay?"

"I hope I can help you take a look at your feelings. But I love you no matter what you are."

You may not believe that anyone could love you if they *really* knew you. And to a degree, you're right—a lot of people can't or won't love you. They'll back off when they find out certain things about you. That's why you don't spill your guts to every person you meet.

Instead, you send out these tests—each one a little more revealing and a little riskier to admit. But you expect the person loving you to flunk the tests.

What are *your* tests? What do you think no one could accept about you? What bombshells do you throw out when someone seems to be getting close to you? What deep, dark secrets do you have that you know no one could tolerate?

Well, guess what! Unconditional love means loving the real you. There are people out there who can love you unconditionally—maybe not your peers because peers have about as much experience with unconditional love as you do. But you've probably caught a glimpse of unconditional love from someone—a parent, a friend's parent, a teacher, a coach, a youth group director, a priest, a counselor, an older friend.

It doesn't mean that these people are perfect at loving without strings attached. They've had their bad days and may even have left you feeling rejected. But they come around! They do their best to show you that you're a worthwhile person—always!

WHAT GOOD IS IT?

By reading this chapter and some of the stories in it, you might be catching on to some of the benefits of unconditional love. But just in case

WHO'S GONNA LOVE ME?

you are feeling a little slow, I thought I would provide you with a few specifics.

> *Benefit 1*
> *Unconditional love provides an emotionally safe place.*

Have you ever gotten mad at a friend but held back because you thought your anger might frighten the friend away? Know what happens to that anger? It goes underground and comes out anyway in the form of gossip, picking on your little brother, or just being in a bad mood.

After meeting with Mrs. Gentry for a while, Eric began to realize that he could loosen up a bit with his feelings. She didn't let him punch holes in the walls or anything like that. But Eric discovered that he could be angry (even at Mrs. Gentry) and voice that anger without scaring her away.

It was okay to be angry, sad, depressed, or to feel dread, apprehension, anxiety—or for that matter, joy, exhilaration, excitement, anticipation. Any emotions were okay in Mrs. Gentry's book. They didn't scare her.

That's emotional safety. You don't feel like you have to hide what you're feeling or even explain it. All you do is *feel* it. You can just run your thoughts and feelings by somebody who is more anxious to help you sort out your feelings than to nail you for them!

LOVE WITHOUT STRINGS

If someone has no strings on you, he or she is going to listen to your emotions. Not that there won't be real consequences if you act on the negative emotions. But emotions are okay. They won't drive a true friend away.

> *Benefit 2*
> *Unconditional love improves*
> *your self-image.*

Messages from others serve as mirrors that reflect back to you what others see in you. If those mirrors are distorted by conditional acceptance, your self-image could also be distorted.

People who accept you only on condition tell you what they *want* to see in you. People who put no conditions on their love tell you what they *do* see in you. The message of unconditional love is perfectly clear—*you are lovable.* You are good just as you are. You have good qualities that can be brought out. You are a good person (even when you have all kinds of negatives floating around).

Remember the sheep and the string. If people tell you long enough and loud enough that you are bad, you will believe it. You will stay in the string—you will follow the conditions. But if people tell you long enough and loud enough that you are good and lovable, you are going to start believing them, too. You are going to start to feel better about yourself. You are going to grow in *confidence,* too. Confidence is believing in *your* goodness and worth (as well as your abilities).

Sound conceited? No way! Conceit is believing you are something that you are *not.* If you believe in your own goodness, you are more likely to believe in the goodness of others. It's not that you are better than others. You just start believing everybody's good!

There is another very special part of this benefit. You might also be able to take criticism better. When somebody points out your weaknesses, you know that underneath it all, you are still good. You know that it is okay to fail—failure doesn't change your basic goodness. In the end, you will see your weaknesses and your strengths—your good points and your bad points—much more clearly.

> *Benefit 3*
> *Unconditional love helps you*
> *love yourself.*

Since the basic message of unconditional love is that you are lovable, you can begin to love yourself, too. If most of your friends accept you conditionally, you've probably been accepting yourself conditionally. Ever have any conversations with yourself in the mirror? Ever hear yourself say anything like this?

LOVE WITHOUT STRINGS

"With a face like that, how can you stand to be seen in public? Why don't you just go back to bed?"

"You dance like a *toad!*"

"She won't like you. You're too short, too weak, and too nerdy." (Actually, it's *you* who doesn't like you.)

If you get enough messages of unconditional love, you might have some pretty good conversations with yourself in the mirror. And eventually, you are going to believe good things about yourself, even when nobody is saying them. You will come to love and accept yourself.

Of course, no one (except God) is perfect at unconditional love. You're bound to get mixed messages, even from the most loving people you know. But if you start looking for relationships without strings, if you stick with people who care about you, you will learn the messages and get the benefits.

But you are going to have to get on the giving end, too. You can't expect somebody to cut the strings and let you run free if you are still putting conditions on your friends.

You are going to have to work on your own attitude. And one of the best ways you can learn how to love is to learn how to party!

Hang around for a while.

This is going to get interesting.

5

PARTY GOD!

■

- Hey! Who is in charge here, anyway?
- What do you make of God? (Or is that the other way around?)
- Nobody likes to party in a messy house.
- Are you trying to tell me that I am supposed to feel good?
- So, where's the party?

WHO'S GONNA LOVE ME?

When all else fails, throw a party. A big party, a little party—who cares? Just throw a party. Nobody will argue with you about the value of a party. But what do parties have to do with your attitude? What do parties have to do with taking the strings off love?

A lot! What is a party? Is it food? drinks? games? music? dancing? talking? singing? Well, a party is probably all those things. But the number one ingredient of a party is people—people gathered together.

Parties are usually *about* something. There are school's-out parties and back-to-school parties. There are birthday parties and anniversary parties. There are we-all-failed-the-math-quiz parties. And let's not forget the just-for-the-heck-of-it parties.

But do you usually have parties with your enemies? Well, no—not usually. Parties are mostly for friends—people who care about one another. The better the friends are, the better the party is.

Think about your best friend for a minute. What is time spent with that person like? What makes being with your best friend so special?

- Beth's best friend, Andrea, helped her when her parents went through a divorce. Andrea listened to Beth's stories long after everyone else stopped listening. She put up with Beth's bad moods and angry outbursts (and there

PARTY GOD!

were a few of those). She seemed to know when Beth needed to talk, to be distracted, to be quiet. During a rough time for Beth, Andrea made the most of their time together.

- Terry always encourages Brian. Brian wants to be an artist. He has talent (but he is worried about sticking to his goal). Well, Terry believes in Brian. So, every time another student puts Brian's work down, or a teacher gives the work a poor grade, Terry is there. He is honest with Brian. (He is quick to point out when Brian is being lazy. But he is just as quick to notice those special touches Brian puts into his work.) Every time Brian is ready to chuck the whole thing, Terry shows up to give Brian a push and to spend some time with him. Maybe that is why Brian gives Terry the credit for the art scholarship he just got.

- Anytime Melissa gets overwhelmed with the daily routine—homework, gossip, the maze of decisions about college—she can count on Valerie to put things together. Valerie is a great talker. She babbles on about her little sister, and how nice it is to see the sun after all that rain, and how good it is to be alive. Valerie gets all the daily stuff done, but she never seems to get down about it. She has a great attitude toward life! She helps Melissa get past the bad stuff and start over fresh.

What is the neatest thing about being with best friends? Best friends are pulling for you. Sometimes you don't feel in charge of your life. Sometimes it feels like you get hit on by parents, teachers, coaches, hall monitors (even God—or so it seems). Best friends sit in your corner. A friend (a really good one) makes it seem that you can be in charge. You can live your life and make it through.

That is why not having a good friend is so scary for people. People without good friends can get pretty lonely. They feel unloved, and it is hard to go out and love somebody else.

A lot of life is spent looking for good friends. And finding friends is not automatic. Don't forget, good friends don't have strings on their love. They accept you—just you.

This is where God comes in. (Stop shaking your head, and follow along.) As I said, God invented unconditional love. God gives unconditional love. And God teaches unconditional love. But let's make sure that we are all talking about God—not somebody we made up.

GOD'S BAD RAP

Remember those messages we get from people—messages that tell us what they are thinking

PARTY GOD!

about us? Remember how people want us to be just like they are—right clothes, right music, right friends, right attitudes about school? Well, a lot of people want God to be just like they are, too. So, they send messages about God.

Some people want God to be the *Boss!* It makes them comfortable knowing that God will always tell them what to do. They need rules, so they have God giving them rules. Of course, they want God to give you the same rules. They are counting on God to set *you* straight.

Other people are looking for God to be their *Judge!* It makes them happy to see God passing out rewards to good people and punishments to bad people. (These same folks are pretty sure who the good people and the bad people are, too.) You can't fool the old Judge! Everything you do will be rewarded or punished. You can count on that. (What a great God!)

Fear can really get people moving. If you have fear of pain and punishment, you just might try to be good. But a God who has you scared stiff all the time doesn't sound like the same God who invented unconditional love—not to me, anyway.

Then there is the *hour-a-week* God. This God shows up at church on Sunday. Everybody gets together for an hour of obligation. A few songs, a few prayers, and the duty is fulfilled for another week. How long would you stick with your best friend if you both felt *you had to* spend one hour a week together—whether you liked it or not! You can have a better relationship with a gas pump!

Now, these images of God are a bad rap. Nobody can relate to a God who punches your time card every Sunday at church, counts the prayers you say and the sins you commit every day, and then hands out big rewards or big demerits—heaven or hell—at the end of it all.

God Is Love

I think it's time to get rid of negative images of God. It is time to get the true image of God. God is a lover—in fact, God *is love*. Put very simply, God is pulling for you, not putting you down. God is teaching you, not testing you. God is building you up, not tearing you down.

Look, you are being tested every day. How much do you know? How much can you do? Who are your friends? Do you dress well enough? Do you have the right things? Do you listen to the right music? Maybe you are even convinced that God is part of the test, too.

Well, I can guarantee you that you will learn a lot more about God by looking at friends and parties than you ever will by buying God's bad rap. Let's just say (for the sake of argument) that God is *Best Friend*. What would that make God in your life?

All of a sudden, this Best Friend shows up everywhere—sitting next to you in English class,

PARTY GOD!

talking with you into the night about almost anything, playing an "air guitar" in your room. God stops being a mean old man in a long white beard. God is neither a man nor a woman—just a friend. God stops floating around a billion miles above the earth. Now God is right there in the middle of things.

Hey, it wasn't God's idea to become a distant, hard-to-reach being way out there. God went to all the trouble of creating a world (a good one, too, remember) to be with you. When Moses asked what name might be a good one for God, God told Moses, "I am the God *who is with you.*"

But God was pretty sure that you and I might need a little more help (okay, *a lot* more help) being friends with God. Enter, Jesus! Jesus is "God in the flesh." Jesus has a human body, human feelings, human needs. Jesus is just the way God made you. But Jesus also tells a lot about God—the Lover.

"Wait a minute, wait a minute, wait a minute! Is this going to be one of those sermons? Jesus will take care of everything, so don't you worry. I thought we were going to talk about parties and having a good time. This is starting to sound like church!"

Hang in there for a while! Stop thinking about Jesus in old ways. Take the chance of looking at Jesus like you never looked at him before. I told you I wasn't going to write baloney—and I am not. But you have to take a

WHO'S GONNA LOVE ME?

couple of risks, too. One of those risks is to look at Jesus in a new way.

Parties, Parties Everywhere

Jesus spent a lot of time at parties. (Oh, yes, he did!) And Jesus went to parties with the strangest people—tax collectors, sinners, prostitutes, the poor, and the outcasts of society. Everybody wanted to have Jesus at their parties.

At a wedding feast in Cana, Jesus felt sorry for the bride and groom because they ran out of wine. So, Jesus saved them from embarrassment and changed water into wine—to keep the party rolling. At a meal with all sorts of important people, Jesus taught that when God throws a party, everybody is invited.

At another party (with his close friends Martha and Mary and Lazarus) Jesus taught that you have to be quiet and listen to the messages of God—they're everywhere. Jesus even gave a party for over five thousand people. They had come to listen to him. They didn't bring anything to eat, so Jesus spread the food around for everybody—bread and fish for the whole gang!

At another party, a woman (everybody knew she was bad news—a real sinner) came up and started washing Jesus' feet. Everybody thought Jesus would really tell her off. But Jesus just looked at the lady and said, "Much will be forgiven you because you have loved much." Can you believe that? Well, neither could the

PARTY GOD!

folks at the party. They were a lot more comfortable with a teacher who would zap sinners. Forgiving people? Outrageous!

Then there was another party—the biggest party of all. Just before Jesus died, he celebrated a meal with his closest friends. At this party, Jesus did some heavy-duty teaching.

Teaching number one: "Wash feet." Jesus got down at the party and washed his friends' feet. Peter got pretty upset about this. But Jesus said, "You call me teacher—and I am that. So, if I (the teacher) get down and wash your feet, you should wash one another's feet." In other words, friends help friends—no matter what.

Teaching number two: "Love one another as I have loved you." At this party, Jesus made a new rule—a new commandment. It sounds simple, just love one another the way Jesus loved. But Jesus loved without any strings. That means the friends of Jesus have to love without strings, too! Good grief—that might be tough.

Teaching number three: "Do this in memory of me!" In other words, when you want to keep Jesus' memory alive, get together and celebrate this *special meal.* (Now, I have heard of parties where everybody tries to get so blasted that they forget all the pain. But Jesus is suggesting that people celebrate to *remember.)*

By the way, this party (called the Last Supper) is loaded with good stuff. If you want to get the whole story, read the last few chapters of Saint John's Gospel. The last few chapters of

Matthew, Mark, and Luke are pretty good, too, if you are interested. The whole message here is very plain. God wants to be where you are. God is pulling for you, challenging you, seeing you through the tough times. Jesus showed, once and for all, that God *believes in you!* God is the best friend ever.

Sometimes you may not feel quite ready for this party kind of God. You are hurting! Then what?

HOW ABOUT A LITTLE HEALING?

What do best friends do for each other? Lots of things, really. They hang out together. They celebrate good times together. They help each other through the bad times. They share secrets. They can even take walks and not say a word to each other. They just seem to know what the other person is thinking and feeling. When times get rough, best friends are *there* for each other.

That's the kind of friendship Jesus has in mind for you. Especially when times get tough, Jesus wants to be there for you. But this friend knows that when things go bad, what you might need most is time to heal. Every relationship needs times of healing and of going on and starting over.

When Beth's parents were getting divorced, Andrea reached out to her to help her heal.

When Terry stood behind Brian, he was helping him go on with his art—go on with using his talent. When Melissa got bogged down with all the heavy stuff in her life, Valerie helped her start over. Valerie made life seem worth living.

A Story in Need of Healing

Just after the Christmas dance (junior year), Jessica fell madly in love with David. She wasn't sure how it happened, but it did. The best thing was that David felt the same way about her. By their second date, they were going steady. (Nobody else seemed right!)

Jes often daydreamed in class. She would touch the beautiful necklace David had given her. She would think about their future together—going to the same college, taking some classes together, talking about other people, planning their future. They would get married (of course) during their last year of college and start a family right after graduation.

What a great plan! Jessica and David spent hours talking—sharing their deepest secrets. They believed in the same things. They even struggled to save sex for their marriage. But their emotions really tied them together. (Or so Jessica thought.)

Toward the end of their senior year, some things started to go wrong. David was getting a lot of pressure from his dad to go to one of the military academies. His parents were fighting (often and bitterly). David kept hearing the same old story. "You're too easy on that boy," shouted Dad.

"You are too hard on him," snapped Mom. David did not know what to think. Mostly, he started to feel like running away. He couldn't even talk about these feelings with Jessica.

As the tension built at home, David started losing interest in school. He became more and more withdrawn—even from Jessica. Jessica tried to be supportive, but she felt David getting more and more distant. Maybe these weren't the biggest problems in the world, but they were sure driving a wedge between Jessica and David.

The two spent less and less time together. Finally, Jessica confronted David. She pointed out how their relationship had gone to pot. (He agreed.) She said they needed to communicate better. (He agreed.) She asked David to let her back in. (He went silent.) She needed to be part of whatever it was that was happening for their relationship to survive. (He agreed and hit her with the real killer.)

Jessica will never forget those words: "We aren't going to make it, Jes." David said them with a straight face. "I think we have to call the whole thing off—forever!" David turned and walked away. David's parents split up. David never went to college. Jessica never had another long talk with him—ever.

Jessica hurt so bad! She needed healing. She had been so open to David. David wasn't out to

PARTY GOD!

get her or anything. But his own problems got dumped at her doorstep.

So, Jessica was angry for letting herself get so vulnerable. She was angry at David for being such a jerk. She was even angry at God. If God is so great, why wasn't everything made right?

Now, if you had stopped Jessica at this moment and told her that Jesus wanted her to party, she just might have spit in your eye. There are a few things standing between Jessica and a good party. Jessica's house is a little too messed up to let a party in. Three things get in her way.

- *Pain.* The hurt of loss is in the way. It is pretty hard to celebrate and feel good about yourself when you are in pain. (And it doesn't make any difference who caused the pain—you could have caused it yourself.)
- *Guilt.* Even though Jessica may have done nothing to cause this breakup, she feels bad for letting herself be vulnerable. Maybe she could have done more. Maybe she wasn't good enough to make things right. It is hard to go on when you feel guilty.
- *Fear.* Remember that old enemy? Well, Jessica is afraid of a lot. She is afraid that every time she sees something that reminds her of David, she will be hurt all over. She is afraid that this might happen again if she falls for somebody

new. She is afraid that she just might be *unlovable.* It is hard to start over when you are afraid.

Healing

Jesus wanted everybody to know that God offers healing. That is why Jesus spent so much time healing all kinds of different people. He cured lepers. He let the blind see. He gave the crippled a chance to walk. He cured little children and old people, too. Everywhere he went there was a message of healing.

Jessica needed healing when David left her. She felt pretty bad about herself. She thought everybody was looking at her and calling her "the one that David dumped." Most of all, she missed her friendship with David. She was more lonely than ever before.

David needed healing, too. He really hurt a friend. He was hurting himself. He needed time to put things back together. He needed time to get over his own pain.

You need healing. All those bad messages, all those big *ifs,* all those conditional acceptances you have gone through have left some pain. The neat thing about life is that it is possible to heal. The neat thing about God is that God is all for healing.

Pain is one of the risks in living. You can be absolutely sure that you will not get through life

PARTY GOD!

without pain. Pain is nature's warning that things are not right. If you have a pain in your mouth, there is a good chance that you have a rotten tooth. If you have a pain in your back, you have a strained muscle (or something like that). When you have a pain in the spirit, you are also getting a warning that things are not right.

You don't cause all your pain, but if you take the risks of living and loving, pain gives the warning that all is not well. But just as there is no excuse for living with a toothache, there is no excuse for living with other pain either.

Here is what the message of Jesus is all about. Want your heart healed? Be open to healing! You can't find healing unless you admit that you hurt. And there is no shame in hurting.

Remember, there are ways to *numb* pain. Drugs, alcohol, and a million other addictions will numb your pain. But none of these things heal your hurt. The message of Jesus is to face the pain and to be open to healing.

Now, is Jesus going to zap you healed? Probably not. Your healing will happen through the ordinary things in your life—through your music, through your friends, through your own quiet times. The big miracle is that healing is possible.

There is this old story about a guy trapped in a flood. He believed that God would save him. He prayed and prayed and prayed, and he was convinced that God would help him.

As he was sitting on his porch, a neighbor in a rowboat came up to the porch. "Hop in, I'll take you to safety."

"Don't worry about me," said the guy. "God will save me. I am sure of it."

The flood waters rose. The man was now hanging out of a second-story window. A police officer came by in a motorboat. "Jump in," said the cop, "and I'll take you to safety."

"Don't worry about me," the fellow said. "God will save me, I am sure of it."

Still the waters rose. Now the guy was standing on the very peak of his roof. Along came a fire department helicopter. The pilot leaned out and shouted, "Grab the line. I will fly you to safety."

"Don't worry about me," said our poor hero. "God will save me. I am sure of it."

Well, the waters rose, and our friend drowned. When he got to heaven, he was really ticked at God. He stormed right up to God and shouted. "Hey, God! I believed in you! I was sure you would save me!"

God looked the guy right in the eye. "What do I have to do? I sent you two boats and a helicopter!"

Everybody likes big miracles. Everybody wants to be healed in one big stroke of God's power. But God likes to work in gentle ways. And God's healing takes some time.

When you hurt, you do want immediate relief. I am sure Jessica wanted to feel better—

now! But healing takes time, and in God's way of running things, healing most often takes place in very ordinary ways. You have to get a new picture of yourself in this, too. You have to believe that you are *worth* healing.

And sometimes you have to ask for help. You have to let people know that you are hurting. People who care about you—people who don't have any strings on their love—will take the time to help.

Going On

No mistakes need be fatal! I said that guilt can keep you from enjoying the party—can keep you from going on. Nobody likes to feel guilty. But everybody has some reason for feeling guilty. You have (I am sure of it) on occasion done something you are ashamed of, sorry for, or just feel stupid about.

David probably had to live with feelings of guilt about dumping Jessica. Everybody needs forgiveness. In fact, forgiveness is the ingredient that makes it possible for life to go on.

Jesus also spent a great deal of his time forgiving people. Nothing was so horrible that Jesus could not forgive it. He forgave the adulterous woman. (Misusing sex can be forgiven.) He forgave the people who put him to death. (Murder can be forgiven.) He told Peter that people should forgive their brothers and sisters seventy times seven times. (It doesn't even make too much of a difference how much you mess up.)

Jesus even told a story about a teenager who took his inheritance and went off and wasted his money. He spent all the cash on getting drunk and on prostitutes. (Not exactly your most charming kind of guy!) He ended up feeding pigs. Well, this wasteful son decides to go home. He is feeling pretty guilty, so he is going to say "I'm sorry" to his father. And then, he is going to ask Dad for a job.

His father sees him coming a long way off. He runs out to meet his son. He doesn't even let him say the "I'm sorry" part. He gives him new clothes and a ring for his finger, and throws him a party! A real bash! And Jesus said that is just how forgiving God is.

So why feel guilty? No need. The creator of unconditional love does not even demand good behavior in order to win this love. Unconditional love forgives! Unconditional love invites you to the party.

So, now there is no reason not to keep going—no reason to stay away from the party.

Starting Over

The hardest thing for Jessica was starting over again with her life. Even when the pain started to go away, even when she got rid of guilty feelings and started to go on with life, she still had a little bit of fear. You see, when you believe the negative messages, it is hard to believe that you are worth a second chance.

There are a lot of people who don't give second chances. Look back at those cliques! You hang around with the wrong people, you're out! You take an interest in the wrong things, you're out. Human beings have a great ability to give "just one chance."

Fortunately, Jesus has a different message. His whole life was about second chances. He gave anybody and everybody the chance to start over. He still gives second chances like they are going out of style.

Jesus knew all about the fears that keep people from starting over. But he gave the biggest lesson in second chances of anybody. The biggest fear anybody has is the fear of death. (I told you we would talk about this later, and we will. But for now, we are talking about starting over.) So Jesus came back from the dead. He rose! (Honest—I didn't make this up either.)

Jesus was saying that in a world of unconditional love, not even death can beat you! You can always start over. Love always gives second chances. Death is clear failure (at least for most people). When Jesus was put to death, his friends were just about ready to cash it in. They were now *really scared!* But Jesus came back into the room and said, "Peace be to you!"

And after he rose from the dead, he had another party. (This one was a beach party. You think I am kidding? Check it out.) Jesus barbecued some fish for his friends and then gave them a challenge. "If you love me, feed my lambs. If you love me, take good care of all my friends! If you love me, love with no strings attached." Please notice that Jesus did not say, "If you feed my lambs, I will love you."

> *Principle 6*
> *Unconditional love heals, forgives, and gives the chance to start over.*

Now, that is something worth celebrating! If you love somebody—truly love somebody—you want to heal that person's pain. You are always ready to forgive the one you love, too. But most of all, if you love without strings, you are always willing to give a second chance. People who love you want *you* to get healing, forgiveness, and a second chance, too. (Even parents sometimes!) When you believe that you are worth healing, that you can be forgiven, and that you can start over, you have your house all ready for a big party!

FEELING GOOD—FEELING BAD

Don't you just hate the words "for your own good"? They are words that often come with

PARTY GOD!

medicine, punishment, discipline ("No, you can't have the car tonight"), and all those good things. You hardly ever think about parties being for your own good.

But God is with you whether you are feeling good or feeling bad. God likes to party.

Let's get something straight. I don't mean unconscious partying. There are people who get unconscious for a whole weekend on alcohol or drugs. They have to check with their friends on Monday to find out if they had a good time. God isn't into that kind of partying.

But God does want you to experience the joy of living as well as the pain of living. God does want you to know that life is *worth* living. Some folks would like you to treat life here on earth like a big test. If you pass it, you go to heaven. Fail it, and you go to hell. There is not much *value* to life here.

God has left messages everywhere that there is a different way of looking at things. Pleasure is not bad! (It isn't everything, but it is most definitely not bad!)

You won't have *pleasure* all the time. But you can have *joy*—even when you are feeling bad. Joy makes people celebrate (life is good!), and joy goes hand in hand with unconditional love.

So, Jesus (whose idea it is to be a best friend and love you unconditionally) just loves experiencing joy with you. As you have seen, Jesus loved to party with his friends.

WHO'S GONNA LOVE ME?

(Okay, now it is time for you to say it: Jesus Christ, *Party God!* That wasn't so hard, was it?)

Does Party God fit any of your images of God? Can you picture Jesus dancing to the latest hit? Can you see Jesus doing a backflip on a skateboard? Can you see Jesus lying in the middle of a field watching the clouds go by? Can you see him running through the field screaming at the top of his lungs?

Can you see Jesus punching out a wall after losing a friend? Can you see him sitting on the curb crying—watching his tears falling on the pavement? Jesus throws "downer" parties after something bad happens. Jesus throws "upper" parties after something good happens.

Jesus Christ knows how to party and wants you to know how to party, too. Jesus throws good parties because you don't have to get smashed or stoned to feel comfortable. This is a party where everybody is welcome—everybody tries to care about others. This is a party with no strings attached. This is a party that lets the joy last long after the pleasure is gone.

Which Way to the Party?

"Is this the commercial? Is this where Father Don passes out Bibles and gets everybody down on their knees? Is this where I find out all the changes I have to make in my life? Is this where I have to start following a whole lot of rules?"

PARTY GOD!

No! Here is the big secret about the invitation to Jesus' party: Be you! That is the trick of unconditional love. It is for *you*—without your masks, without your games, without any big talk, without any big success (or big rebellion).

Here is another secret: You can find the Party God right in your life and in the relationships you have. You have heard about a ton of relationships in this book already. Karen and Carolyn, Eric and Mrs. Gentry, me and my coach and my high school teacher—a whole lot of them. Right in the middle of all those relationships is Jesus—the Party God.

So, the party is where you are now! You don't have to be somebody you are not. You don't have to put on a long face and look religious. You don't have to *do* anything. You just have to *be* yourself—your best self. And you have to let other people be themselves, too.

How do you get to go to a party? You get an invitation. And every day, in the little things that are all a part of your life, you are getting an invitation from the Party God! The invitation is very simple—keep the party going. Keep the message of love going. Heal, forgive, be ready for the second chance.

There is a line at the bottom of the invitation, too: *B.Y.O.B.* (That does not mean "Bring your own bottle!") What it means is "Bring your own best—your own best self!" That's what this Party God is looking for.

Now, if it is all the same to you, let's party!

6

TRUTH AND CONSEQUENCES

■

- Am I free to be me?
- Love me enough to let me feel the way I feel!
- I hate to say "I told you so," but I told you so (at least fifty times)!
- Setting limits is one of those things that parents do best.
- I believe in a God who is in the flesh—right here and right now!

WHO'S GONNA LOVE ME?

Guess what! There is another principle of unconditional love. (I didn't think it was such a good idea to give you all the principles at once. That's why I split them up a bit.) I thought this particular principle deserved a chapter all to itself. It is pretty important. It says a lot about what makes you tick—about what is best in you.

> *Principle 7*
> *Unconditional love does not take away free will.*

Everybody wants to be free. Wars have been fought over freedom. (And a lot of the fights you have with your parents have a bit to do with freedom, too.) You can get all sorts of invitations to the party, but you have to *accept* the invitations—freely. God is not going to force you to come to the party.

This principle is simple enough. But you may have some objections to the principle as I've stated it:

- "Yes, but my parents take away my free will. They certainly don't let me do whatever I want."
- "Yes, but God knows everything that's going to happen. So we don't really have free will."
- "Yes, but with all the laws, rules, and

regulations, we might just as well not have free will. We sure can't *use* it."
- "So, I am free! What about the consequences of my choices and my actions?"

That did it! That is the very objection I was waiting for. What about the consequences? In North America, we have this strange notion that free will and consequences should be separate issues.

And why not? How many so-called friends out there will help you cheat if you didn't study for a test? How many times on television cop shows do parents come in and lie for their kid? "He can't be the ax murderer, officer. He was with me, drinking warm milk before bed."

How many vandals do you see scrubbing the walls where they had spray-painted some graffiti? Not too many. How many parents have even said to their kids, "Just make sure you don't get caught"?

And how many times has a student said a prayer like this: "Dear God, I know I should have started this report three months ago like the teacher said to, but the darn thing is due tomorrow. I need your help. Let me understand the information from these ten books and write this ten–page paper in an hour. Okay, I'll accept two hours. But that's my final offer." And God gets the blame when the report doesn't get finished!

Ever get mad at a friend who wouldn't help you cheat? Ever get angry at a teacher because you failed a test (one you didn't study for)? Ever get mad at your parents for not giving you the car (even though you have a moving violation on your record)? Ever lose a license for reckless driving? How silly!

We like to think that actions and consequences don't *have* to go together. But they do.

FOR EVERY ACTION!

Let me think out loud for a minute. What if consequences and actions really didn't relate to one another? I could stick my hand in a fire and not get burned. I could watch television all night and not get tired. I could eat all the food I wanted and not get fat. I could overdose on drugs and not die.

But then studying wouldn't necessarily make me any smarter. Working out wouldn't make me more muscular. Those are consequences of actions, too. If actions and consequences don't go together, those things wouldn't necessarily go together either.

In fact, you'd have no control over what happened to you because whatever happened to you would be totally unrelated to your actions. So what's the point of doing anything? There wouldn't even be a point to watching a funny

TRUTH AND CONSEQUENCES

movie because it wouldn't necessarily make you laugh. There would be no point in living.

Luckily, you do have control over what happens to you. You study, you get good grades (at least okay grades). You practice basketball five hours a day, you get to be a pretty good basketball player. You do drugs, you fry your brain. (Your choice! Your control!)

Many actions have more than one consequence. Some consequences might be good, some might be bad. What you try to do (most of the time) is choose actions that result in good consequences and minimize the bad consequences. One of the hardest lessons to learn in life (and most of us have to learn it several times before we get it right) is that actions have consequences. What I choose will affect others! There is no such thing as a choice without a result, or consequence!

If you choose to have sex with someone, you open yourself to possible pregnancy or strong emotional ties with another person. If you choose to steal from a store (besides the risk of getting caught), you have hurt somebody's balance sheet and have made other customers pay more. If you pretend to love somebody you don't care for, your dishonesty will sooner or later hurt that person—and hurt you!

Bottom line? If you really want to be free—really be you—you have to take responsibility for your actions and the consequences of those actions. You can't pretend. If you are pretending, you have put strings on *yourself*—you have begun to make yourself unlovable! Ouch!

Feelings Are Real

How do you feel? Do you feel free? Do you feel happy, sad, scared, lonely, angry, excited, nervous? Your emotions are also consequences of actions (yours and others). You want to ask somebody to dance, you feel nervous. You think about your best friend moving away, you feel sad. Pass the test (or daydream about passing it), you feel happy.

When feelings come from thoughts and not actions, you can handle them pretty easily (most of the time). If the feelings are bad ones, distract yourself—think of something else. Get involved in something. Pretty soon, the feelings go away.

But what about emotions that result from actions? You cheat on a test. You feel regret and embarrassment. Your friend does move away. You feel lonely and afraid. The temptation is to try to hide these feelings, too. You try to distract yourself from your real feelings. But the distraction doesn't work—not for long. Unless you face those feelings, the feelings will come back to haunt you.

It's what Jessica went through after David broke up with her. The emotions she felt were the consequences of an action. If she had tried to ignore her feelings, they would have come back anyway. Instead, she faced them and dealt with them. Eventually, Jessica healed—the terrible feelings went away.

How you feel is important! If you choose to ignore your feelings, your feelings will get jumbled up and confused. You get angry at a friend who lied to you. But you try to ignore the feelings. (Maybe you are afraid you'll lose your friend.) Two days later, you scream at your little brother for bumping your stereo. Or maybe you get depressed. Depression is a funny, secondary feeling. It is a sign that you just might not be facing some real strong emotion.

Maybe you think anger is bad. So you start feeling guilty after feeling angry. Those guilty feelings are secondary feelings, too.

Remember, it's not the first feelings that are destructive. The secondary ones—depression and guilt and anxiety—can be. If you feel bad because something bad has happened, that is just the way it is supposed to be. If you feel bad about feeling bad, that is really crippling.

If a friend of yours commits suicide, you ought to feel bad! In fact, you ought to get with other friends and feel bad together. You need to face the bad feelings caused by your friend's suicide—and *celebrate* those feelings.

Let those first feelings come out, and you can deal with them. Hide them, and you get hurt—you are not free. It can be scary sometimes. You may be afraid you're going to hurt somebody if you allow yourself to feel anger. Or you may be afraid of never feeling good again if you let yourself feel sad. But emotions are real. They are supposed to be felt. If you let yourself feel, the feelings will eventually die down and even go away.

Somebody who loves you without any strings is willing to let you be free to feel. That is all part of this principle of letting you have free will. "I will love you only if you feel the way I want you to feel" is a very big *if*.

Face the Music!

Doug invited Rachel on a camping trip—just the two of them. Rachel was pretty sure what Doug had in mind. He wanted to sleep with her. The camping trip was just the opportunity. Rachel was quite proud that somebody like Doug was interested in her. She was tempted. She could make up a story for her parents. This could be fun. But she thought she might just talk over the trip with her friend Sarah.

Sarah had heard that Doug is a love-'em-and-leave-'em guy. She wasn't too thrilled when Rachel started dating Doug, but she stuck with Rachel. She was nice to Doug when the three of them were together. She even acknowledged that some good things had come of the relationship.

During the conversation, Sarah warned Rachel about Doug's reputation. She also made her own principles about sex before marriage quite clear. But Sarah also listened to Rachel talk about

TRUTH AND CONSEQUENCES

the positive stuff in the relationship with Doug. Doug had talked with Rachel about his reputation and told her that he was tired of shallow relationships—that he *loved* Rachel.

Well, Sarah helped Rachel sort out the pros and cons of going. She let her opinion be known, but she also let Rachel know that only Rachel could decide what to do.

Rachel went on the trip. The inevitable happened! What fun! She and Doug had a very *good* time. It was great! She came back happy—and full of love. But even on the way home Doug started to act differently. Within a month, he dropped Rachel.

Back to Sarah! How did Sarah handle this one? Did she say, "I told you so, dummy!" and really rub it in? No, instead, Sarah listened. Sarah gave Rachel a shoulder to cry on. Sarah gave Rachel a chance to check out the consequences of what she had done.

That's love without strings! First, Sarah helped Rachel sort out the possible consequences of her decision—the good and the bad. But she did not try to make the decision *for* Rachel. After Rachel made her choices and got hit with the consequences, Sarah did not judge. She did not try to rescue Rachel. She did not make light of Rachel's feelings. Instead, she gave Rachel the opportunity for a second chance.

Bottom line: Sarah believed in Rachel enough to let her make her own decision *and* to deal with the consequences.

What would Sarah's message have been if she had tried to make the decision *for* Rachel? "You're not capable of handling such a major decision, so I'll handle it for you. You're too immature, too weak, too confused to do this yourself."

People who love you without strings also believe in you. They believe in your ability to handle whatever comes your way. They believe you will look for the help you need. They are there to offer whatever help and support they can. And they will allow you to choose for yourself. But they will also be there to help you pick up the pieces!

Setting Limits

"Just a darn minute! My parents are *always* trying to make decisions for me. They are just loaded with 'thou-shalt-nots.' Does that mean that my *parents* are flunking out in the unconditional love department?"

Oh, sure, some parents *do* try to keep their children down—never letting them spread their wings. But most parents are trying to do what is best for their families. And if you let anybody live your life *for* you, you are not using your free will.

But don't confuse limits with a lack of freedom. Every parent sets limits! (And unless you are spoiled rotten, you have quite a few limits in your life. Am I right?)

TRUTH AND CONSEQUENCES

Free will works best within limits. If you could choose absolutely anything, at absolutely anytime, you would have a tough time choosing at all. God did not give you a vote in choosing your parents. You were not asked your opinion on the color of your skin, your height, the texture of your hair. You can decide till midnight not to have pimples, but the choosing doesn't help much.

Now, you can choose to drive under the influence. But parents (and the whole of society) will cream you if they catch you doing that. Why? Because the consequences of that action can be (and very often are) disastrous. So, society has set a limit: Driving drunk is a crime.

Let's get back to parents. Parents have a responsibility to you and to society for you. (That is why when *you* trash somebody's house at a party, your parents have to pay the bills. Any wonder they set limits?) They carry out that responsibility by making rules—setting limits. You break those rules—step over those limits—and they have some consequences waiting for you. You stay out all night without permission? You are grounded for three months!

"Nice try, Father Don! But those are really strings. If my parents loved me, they would trust me. If they loved me, they wouldn't be in my face all the time. If they cared about me, they would let me do my own thing. Right?"

Wrong! Now who is spouting the big *ifs?* Those last three sentences were about the strings

WHO'S GONNA LOVE ME?

you have on *your* love—not the strings your parents have on you.

Here is the big difference: People put strings on their love (conditions) in order to control you—make you act the way they want you to act. You have to fulfill the conditions or you just won't get the love. Good parents (and I know there are bad parents, too) already love you. They are setting limits *because* of their love.

The Apple Snack

This is the way God (the inventor of unconditional love) handles things, too. Take, for example, the story of Adam and Eve in the Bible. (I don't want to get into any of those arguments about whether the "apple" was real, or how this happened. The story is a good story, so just look at it like that.) This story is a story of limits and a story of love.

God created Adam and Eve and put them in a beautiful garden. Everything was wonderful. The two of them "walked with God." They named animals. They had tons of good things to eat. They were happy as clams. (Does anybody know why *clams* are supposed to be so happy?)

But God set a limit. "Don't eat from the Tree of the Knowledge of Good and Evil. If you do, you will die!" Simple enough limit. God loved Eve and Adam. As part of that love, God wanted the couple to have the choice to love

TRUTH AND CONSEQUENCES

back. God did not want toys. God wanted a *relationship.* In a relationship with God, Adam and Eve learned a lot about goodness. But the temptation to step over the limit was strong.

They knew that God was just terrific, but what was on the other side of this big limit? Evil? A chance to be better than God? Hmmmm!

God gave out free will. But God also dished up some guidance. Adam and Eve were well informed about the consequences: "Eat from that tree, and you are doomed to die."

God didn't love poor Adam and Eve any less. Do your parents love you less when they say, "Please don't drink that bottle of liquid Drano. If you do, you will die"? God did not want the couple to stay away from the tree to *earn* God's love! God's love set the limit.

Well, Adam and Eve ate from the tree. Adam blamed Eve. Eve blamed the serpent. The rest is history (you know what I mean). Adam and Eve dealt with the consequences, and the rest of us deal with the consequences, too. Enter evil!

The Devil Made Me Do It!

In case you haven't noticed, evil is a very real part of life. Evil is like a giant curtain hiding God from everybody. In the Old Testament, God spends a lot of time helping people rediscover good. God gathers a people. God delivers people from slavery. God gives a full set of limits—

WHO'S GONNA LOVE ME?

guidelines! (Okay, let's call them what they are—*commandments.*)

It is pretty cozy to blame Adam and Eve and their wrong choice of fruit for all this mess. First two human beings do wrong, and everything went downhill after that. A lot of people like to think that when Adam and Eve were shown the door of Paradise, human nature went bad. Nobody was any darn good. Everybody was evil as sin. God got disgusted. God took away that good old unconditional love and started putting strings on love. (Chalk up a victory for the Devil!)

Now there is this picture of God beating on human beings. "I will love you if . . . ," shouts this angry God! So, now God is saying the biggest *if* of all.

I don't think God stops loving people for a split second. People step over limits. People choose to do what is evil. People misuse their free will. But in the middle of all this is the loving God. God is a little harder to see now. We get so caught up in stepping over limits that we forget God loves without strings. We like to think God puts conditions on love because *we* like to put conditions on love.

If God puts strings on love, what happens to you? You are now on the outs with God *unless* you fulfill the conditions. You are a bad person! You aren't worth a bit unless you behave. And God gets farther and farther away. God goes back to being Boss and Judge and Rule Maker.

You go back to following orders, waiting to get zapped, and trying to win God's love.

Not a very pretty picture, is it?

GOD IS WITH YOU

Well, I don't think the picture is true. In that picture, God comes into the flesh in Jesus to whip you into shape, to give you new conditions, to save you from bad choices, to take away your freedom. But Jesus didn't come that way. Jesus came helpless, healing, telling stories, forgiving, giving second chances.

Jesus became flesh to show how much God loves, not to invent new tests for you. You have enough tests and conditions in your life. If Jesus is around to test you some more, what kind of friend is he? Jesus is around to pull back the curtain—to show just how much unconditional love God has for you.

(You do not have to buy this right now. I just want you to think about it. Let this message soak in. If you can really begin to see the messages of love, you are coming a long way to answering the question on the cover of this book.)

Remember the tests we give people who show us unconditional love. ("Would you love me if I were gay? Would you love me if I were a bad student? Would you love me if I ignored you?") Jesus passed all the tests—even the biggest test. "Would you love me if it meant you had to die for me?" Answer? "You bet!"

And the curtain came tumbling down! Look! God really does love me. What a kick!

People say, "Jesus died for your sins." Well, that is true. But here is what that means. Jesus died to show God's love—which forgives all your sins, your selfishness, your conditions—everything. Jesus makes it easier for you to have a relationship with God. (And relationship is what this book is about.) Jesus' death didn't *force* God to forgive. His death *shows* how loving and forgiving God is.

The Big Choice

Now you can choose to have a relationship with God. You can choose to love. That is what free will is all about. It isn't freedom from consequences. It isn't freedom to do anything you want anytime you want. God gave you free will so that you can say "I love you." And God gave free will so you can hear somebody else say "I love you" to *you!*

You have the ability to choose love! That is just about the best gift ever. It is the biggest choice ever, too. You can also choose *not* to love.

"Here comes the commercial!"

Right! But the commercial is not about Bibles and kneeling in church and spouting prayers. The commercial is about choosing to

TRUTH AND CONSEQUENCES

love—God, Jesus, friends, parents, teachers, yourself.

By the way, I take Jesus very, very seriously (even as a Party God). Jesus is real and Jesus is around. I am not ashamed to admit that I love Jesus and Jesus loves me. (Nothing embarrassing about that—at all!)

Has anybody ever told you that it is stupid to believe in or to love God—or Jesus? Why did they say that? Why would anybody want you to close your heart to something? Why would anybody want to keep you from looking at God in a new way? Why would they make a condition of you *not* having Jesus as a friend part of their acceptance of you? I have never been able to figure that out.

Remember, the freedom to love is not a magic trick. You will probably not start seeing visions of angels. You will not start sounding like a preacher. You probably won't even start acting strange. But the choice to love will change you—radically.

By the way, before you give up on the idea of a personal friendship with Jesus, why not give it a try? You might enjoy being with God in the flesh—right here and right now.

I hope you enjoy being a lover!

7

WHO ME? A LOVER?

- Do you mean that I am going to have to learn how to love? (You sneaked that one up on me!)
- Loving is not automatic!
- I find it very hard to take off my masks.
- The biggest fear? I am scared to death—of dying.
- There are so many people to love—and so many ways to love them.

WHO'S GONNA LOVE ME?

Let's go back to the story of Jessica and David for a minute. It had a pretty sad ending, but I want to go back before the end—back when Jessica and David were still very much in love and still had plans. When the two of them were still in love, they had a lot of energy for relationships. Other friendships, even acquaintances, looked good.

Jessica was a better listener when she was in love. She seemed more patient and more optimistic. She felt more alive, and her friends remarked that she was more fun to be with than she was before she started seeing David.

One of the best things about unconditional love? It is contagious. When you know you are loved unconditionally (no strings and no big *ifs*), you find it a lot easier to love others. You are more willing to reach out to others.

One very hot day, Jesus was journeying through Samaria (one of the northern areas of Palestine). He stopped by a well to rest and get a drink. A woman came to get some water from the well. Jesus asked the woman for a drink.

The woman thought this kind of silly. First of all, she was suspicious. Second, Jesus was a Jew. (Jews did not get along with Samaritans.)

Jesus said, "If you knew who was asking you for a drink, you might ask him for a drink of living water. Whoever drinks the water I give will never be thirsty."

Well, this threw the Samaritan woman. She did not have the slightest idea what this living

WHO ME? A LOVER?

water was all about. But here is the point. When you enter good relationships—relationships based on love without strings—you don't run dry. You don't get selfish. You don't get mean. You get better.

What Jesus was offering the woman at the well was unconditional love—his love. And that love would make her day.

The amazing thing is that loving others brings even more joy to your life than *being* loved does. Loving others brings joy to you. But it also brings growth and (I know how you hate this word) maturity. The more mature you are, the easier it is for you to focus on other people's needs—to put your own needs on hold.

Be careful! You do need love yourself. You need to tap into that living water—real unconditional love. You have to be open to *being* loved just for yourself.

TRY WALKING ON WATER

Do you remember learning how to ride a bicycle or a skateboard? Remember the times you went too fast, leaned too far to one side, hit a bump, or took the corner too quickly? Wipeout!

Did it matter? It hurt at the time. (And that skinned knee looked pretty ugly.) But did you stop riding forever? Did you say, "I'll ride again when I am absolutely sure I will never wipe out again!" Wiping out isn't a great experience. But you can't become a skilled bike rider or skateboarder without running the risk of the wipeout.

There is one way to guarantee that you won't fail. Don't try. (Of course, you won't succeed either.) There is a story in the Gospels about trying and failing. The story stars the Apostle Peter—the most impulsive of Jesus' friends. Peter would try anything once. Jesus said, "Come, follow me!" Peter followed. If Jesus tried something, Peter had to try it, too.

One night, during a storm, Jesus came walking up to the Apostles' boat. (I did say walking—right over the water.) When Peter saw that it was Jesus and not some ghost, he had to try this, too. So, Peter jumped out of the boat and started walking toward Jesus.

Maybe it started to hit him that he was walking on water. Maybe he just chickened out. Anyway, Peter started to sink. "How about a hand here, Lord?" cried Peter. Of course, Jesus grabbed Peter and pulled him up.

Now there were another eleven Apostles sitting in the boat thinking that Peter was crazy. They were safe in the boat—and that is just where they were going to stay. Not Peter! He had to try. When you read the Gospels (and the Acts of the Apostles), you find out that Peter made a habit of failing. But that is because Peter made a habit of *trying*. When it comes to loving, everybody has to play Peter. If you stay in the boat, you will be safe. You have to take the risk of walking on some pretty rough water to become a lover. But ask Peter—it is worth the risk.

It can be noted that Jesus was right there—ready to catch Peter when he started to sink. The lesson of Peter getting grabbed by Jesus is that even on the tricky waters of love, mistakes are not fatal.

Jesus is not pulling for you to fail. But you will make mistakes—maybe even wipe out. But if you are risking for love, you will get grabbed. Jesus will see to it that you don't drown.

Don't expect that you will be 100 percent consistent in loving. You are not going to cut all the strings out of loving today (and probably not for a long time to come). You are going to have bad days. But the gift Jesus gives is not consistency—the gift is love.

Here is a tip. The more you love yourself, the easier it is to love others. As you love yourself more, the less afraid you are of failing, of looking foolish, of risking things you have never done before. It becomes more and more natural to take the big *ifs* off your love.

THE MASQUERADE PARTY

Costume parties are fun. You get to dress up like a rock star, a comic-book character, a historical figure, or some other crazy thing. Nobody knows who is hiding in the costume. The big

WHO'S GONNA LOVE ME?

fun is trying to guess everybody's true identity. It is also fun to try to figure out *why* people chose the disguises they did.

But the Party God is not inviting people to a masquerade party. Unconditional love does not hide behind masks. It does not play games with people's hearts.

Tim was the "class clown." Every class has one (at least). He could turn anything into a joke. Everybody said Tim was great fun to be with. He was the life of the party. But Tim was wearing a clown mask to the party. The mask saved Tim the risk of really listening—really participating in the group.

As time wore on, Tim got a little tired of his clown mask. A week after Carla failed the history exam, Tim realized how much he had teased Carla. Maybe that teasing had gone too far.

A few days later (daydreaming in biology class), Tim flashed on a very sad look on Joe's face. Joe had tried to talk to Tim that morning. Tim just made a joke and walked on. (Joe looked hurt.)

But Marcus! Marcus was Tim's very best friend. Marcus had just broken up with Nancy. He came to Tim for support. Tim had a great time with this. His clown act was never better. Marcus gave a nervous grin or two. But Marcus didn't come back for more.

Now the clown mask started to pinch. That day after school, Tim looked for Marcus. He

WHO ME? A LOVER?

walked up and asked Marcus how he felt about Nancy. Marcus thought Tim was going to come at him with some more comedy. So, he kidded around a bit. Tim just listened—and kept listening. Pretty soon, Marcus opened up to Tim. He told him the whole story. The mask was off. Tim took the risk. And Marcus felt he had a friend who cared.

To take off your mask, you have to learn to break old habits. You probably put on your mask automatically. I can't even begin to tell you what your mask looks like. But you know. You know right now. And what is more, you will know for sure the next time you wear it to avoid the risk of loving.

You want to be the best you—just like Tim did. But God's Spirit sometimes has a tough time getting through. The Spirit got through to Tim by letting him flash on the effects his mask had on others and on himself. The signs were right in front of Tim. No thunder, no lightning—just that flash inside that said, "Tim, your clown act is turning you into a jerk. Stop it!"

Tim did not wallow around in guilt. (He could have, and maybe he even did in real life, but for the purposes of keeping his story short, I got right to the point.) Instead, Tim zeroed in on positive behavior.

Losing a bad habit is like trying to lose weight. If you sit around all day and think about the fact that you are on a diet, you will eat before nightfall. If you spend the day focusing on other activities you have planned, you will get to the end of the day and shout, "Hey! I did it! I really did it!"

Tim focused on listening. Because he took the risk and went out to Marcus, he could say to himself, "Hey, I didn't clown around!" Tim *will* clown around again—bet on it! Even though he wears a clown mask, Tim is a truly funny guy. But maybe Tim can say, "I didn't use my clowning around to hide from anything today!" Wouldn't that be great!

In the process of taking off your mask, you will probably find yourself right in the middle of doing just what you are trying to stop! Well, then, stop. Correct the course. Get on target. Get out from behind the mask. Every time you break the routine, you improve. You will start doing the loving thing. And (trust me) it will feel great.

(Just a quick reminder. People who accept you conditionally do not want you to change. If you start pulling off your mask in front of them, they will make you put it right back on. You may have to face the fact that the people you think are on your side just might be the ones who will keep you at the masquerade party—forever.)

I haven't asked you to stick your thumb in this book for a while, have I? Well, you might want to do it again right now. Close your eyes and think about the things you hide behind, the masks you wear, the games you play. What can you do about them? What would you like to do

WHO ME? A LOVER?

about them? Who can help you leave the masquerade party and take the risk of love?

THE GREATEST FEAR OF ALL

You got your mask—your bad habits—in the first place because of fear. Remember the fear of rejection, the fear of pain, and the fear of failure? These fears can get anybody in trouble.

- *Fear of rejection:* You got so scared you were going to be alone that you decided to wear any mask you needed to be accepted. You took fewer and fewer risks because one false step and your clique would send you packing. Here is the beginning fear—the fear of not belonging.
- *Fear of pain:* Look, this fear never goes away. Nobody likes pain. But because you couldn't face pain—couldn't work it into your life—you avoided it. You wrapped yourself up in false fronts. You hid in your room. You stuck with your books, your music, your television, and maybe a group who protected you. Now you are frozen. You don't want to hurt. You are afraid to hurt.
- *Fear of failure:* Aim at nothing and you will hit it! If you had aimed too high, and you had missed, the world would

know you as a failure. So you went for the comfort zone. You did not stretch yourself. You took the easy road. Or maybe you took the compulsive road. You stomped over everybody in your path to succeed.

Just about every story in this book looked at one of those three fears. Don't be surprised if you find those fears in yourself—everybody has them. The big question is "Will I let those fears stop me in my tracks?"

The Gospels have a lot to say about those fears, too. The whole life of Jesus (I hope you read the Gospels sometime—cover to cover) is filled with rejection and pain and failure. Jesus was supposed to be the Promised One of God. What did he get for it? Rejection by the people he came to teach and love, torture at the hands of the holiest people in town, and complete failing grades—even from some of his closest friends. (There is a lesson in there somewhere.)

You can't make it through life without facing those three fears. You won't make it through life without facing the biggest fear of all—*the fear of death.*

Teach Me to Die

A major cause of death in teenagers is suicide. Hundreds (even thousands) of teenagers are so afraid of life, they check out. If you have ever

WHO ME? A LOVER?

felt suicidal, you know what the fear of death is all about—what the fear of life is all about. Learning how to die has *nothing* to do with suicide—at all.

There is a trick to this: To learn how to die, you need to learn how to live! Death is ending one life to begin another—a new life! Suicide is a feeble attempt to end *everything!* It is an attempt to numb pain *forever.*

There is nothing wrong with *feeling* suicidal. Fear can give you those feelings. But if you feel them, do me and yourself a big favor—*tell somebody!* Don't give hints because a lot of us are not that sharp. Come right out with it. Say, "I am feeling like killing myself." There are a lot of people in your life—teachers, priests, ministers, counselors, parents, friends—who *will* listen. But don't force them to read your mind.

Now back to the fear of death. You are going to die. I am going to die. All God's children are going to die! The *big death*—no more breath in the body—happens only once. But parts of you die every day.

That is where the fear comes in. When you were a little kid, maybe your first hint of death was the dead hamster in the cage. You looked in and thought your little friend was sleeping. You poked. Nothing happened. All of a sudden it hit you. Great big tears filled your eyes. Your mouth dropped open. You cried—even screamed, "Mommy, Daddy, Harvy is *dead!*"

WHO'S GONNA LOVE ME?

Maybe your next experience of death was Grandma or Mom or Dad. Maybe a friend moved away and you never heard from her again. Maybe you saw one last fight between your mom and your dad—the door closed and one of them was out of your life.

That's when it hit you. This love stuff doesn't last. Pets don't last. Grandparents don't last. Parents don't last. Nothing—*not even me*—lasts. Who wouldn't be afraid.

Listen to the top ten songs on the charts today. How many of them talk about death—either the big *D* or all the little deaths? How many of them talk about hoping for something that lasts forever? How many of them talk about the fear of parting (that is also a death fear)?

Your fear is well founded. But if you are controlled by the fear of death, you will miss all the growing time between birth and death. (And you will be ill prepared for the new life that is promised after death.)

No doubt somebody told you about the caterpillar. The fuzzy green worm wraps itself up in a cocoon. It gets all crusty. Then, in spring, the little fellow bursts out of the cocoon. It has become a wonderful butterfly.

Jesus talked about a grain of wheat. "Unless a grain of wheat falls to the ground and dies, it stays just a grain of wheat. But if it dies, it produces a whole crop!"

Those are figures of speech—examples. They are supposed to explain death. They are

WHO ME? A LOVER?

supposed to help you move ahead with your life—to change and grow. But if you are controlled by the fear of death, you will tend to keep making the same safe mistakes over and over again. You will be afraid to break old habits.

Death is a great mystery. Nobody knows for sure what lies on the other side of death. But one of the messages of Jesus—one of the great events of unconditional love—is that death means "new life." Every time you make a choice, you sacrifice something. Decide to become a doctor, you may need to sacrifice the chance to be a model. Decide to become a figure skater, you sacrifice hours and hours of time and a chance for a normal social life.

But on the other side of every sacrifice is something very, very new—a new you. If you sacrifice your old games, your old masks, your old habits, you may find a new you on the other side.

I feel certain that there is life after death because in my life there has been so much life after all my little deaths. My little deaths were not always so peaceful. Sometimes I went kicking and screaming. But I feel that all the little deaths are teaching me a lot about the death I still face—the final passage out of this life.

Everybody needs to learn how to die. But look around you. A lot of people are trying to hide from death. There are two ways to run away from death.

- Make light of life. Try to forget that life is sacred and precious. Pretend that life is one big shoot-'em-up with bodies everywhere. Pretend that life is just a big game with no rules. Survival is part of the game.
- Deny death. Pretend that death will happen to everybody but you. Pretend that you are safe from death. Don't take any risks in life or in love—just take the easy course. Blame God for anything wrong with the world.

But even if you run like hell, you can't beat death. A fairly young college professor (he was fifty, but that is starting to look younger to me all the time) came down with amyotrophic lateral sclerosis—Lou Gehrig's disease. He was a scholar. His students loved him. He had traveled the world over. He was athletic and competitive. But this disease didn't ask what a nice guy he was. He was going to die from the disease in six months.

Somebody from the ALS Society came to his hospital room to interview him. One of the questions she asked was "You are dying of ALS. What did God have to do with your disease?"

His answer was not what you might expect. "My disease is real," he said. "The virus or germ that caused it is floating around in the air. I caught it. I don't think God had anything at all to do with giving me this disease. But I believe

WHO ME? A LOVER?

God has *everything* to do with the way I handle it."

"What do you think of God?" asked the young lady.

"I have traveled throughout the world," said the professor. "Everywhere I have seen evidence of the reality called God—Buddha, Krishna, Allah, Muhammad, Jesus. Right now, my image of God is the one found in the Gospel story of the Prodigal Son. I see God with arms outstretched—waiting to welcome me home forever."

The biggest part of dying is letting go. If you learn to let go—a little bit every day—you will learn how to die. If you let go of your anger to forgive somebody who hurt you, you are learning how to die. If you let go of your pride and your fear to risk loving somebody, you are learning to die. If you let go of your mask to be your real self, you are learning to die.

But most important, you are learning to live and to love.

LOVE WHILE THE SUN SHINES!

You may not overcome all your fears today (or next week, for that matter). But you can start being a lover today. The first thing you are going to notice as you accept the title of lover is that there are a lot of people out there to love—

billions of them. Can you love them all? Of course, but not all in the same way.

Peers

You have hung around with the same crowd for a while (if you haven't been moving around too much). This crowd you travel with is made up of your peers. How can you go about loving these people? How can you love people outside this immediate circle?

Remember, you don't love whole groups of people. You love individuals. You are certainly closer to some of your friends than you are to others. There is nothing wrong with that. It is not possible (or even a good idea) to have close, revealing relationships with everyone you meet.

Look at the way you relate in your circle of friends and with each individual in the group. The most important thing for you to do is to stop playing games here. This is the area in your life that probably has the highest level of *conditional* acceptance—the most strings. The best way to cut the strings is to be yourself. You may not have to share your darkest secrets, but don't let your circle of friends become a masquerade. Don't wear a mask.

Notice how you hide in the group. Try to break old habits. Start making changes—little ones in the way you react. When Tim, the clown, took off his mask, he was better able to offer Marcus healing and a second chance. He

WHO ME? A LOVER?

didn't try to take away the pain, but he was there for support and encouragement. So the best way to start loving your peers without strings? Be *there* for them!

If you have a friendship with Jesus, you can let this dribble into your relationship with your peers. How? The way Jesus suggested it. Jesus did not give all his friends pulpits to preach from. So, don't *tell* your peers about God and love and Jesus. Show them!

Jesus is not big on talk. He is big on action. "This is how people will know that you are my friends," Jesus said, "you love one another."

"What? Are you trying to tell me that *actions* speak louder than words here?"

Absolutely! Right now you are at a stage of your life when you travel with the pack. The group is very important to you. Your peers make up most of the relationships in your life. This is good, and it is important. This is how you get ready for adult life.

But you will stay an adolescent until you learn to think, act, and decide for yourself. You need to practice acting for yourself—even in the way you love the members of your peer group. And so, actions do speak louder than words in the group.

To grow in your ability to love your peers, you have to start cutting away the strings. Get involved with your friends. Don't take away their right to make decisions for themselves. Let your friends suffer or enjoy the consequences of their decisions. Stand by for healing, forgiveness, and second chances. Don't forget to seek forgiveness when you hurt a friend.

When friendship starts to hurt and to cost, that is when it starts to get most real. Friendship is not always a question of feeling good. It is a matter of giving—whatever is needed. And sometimes it isn't easy to give.

Get ready for some rejection with your peers, too. Some people may not be ready for the real you. Some people may not be ready to take off their masks. Your love may not be welcome.

But be prepared to party! Celebrate with your friends. Celebrate successes and failures, good times and bad times. Jesus Christ—Party God—wants to celebrate with you and with your friends.

Boyfriend/Girlfriend

In no kind of relationship are more games played and more masks worn than in the romantic relationship between a boy and a girl—man and woman—male and female! Why this is so is always a mystery to me. (Well, maybe it isn't such a great mystery after all. Sexual emotions are some of the most powerful we have. And it is very easy to separate sex from love! It is done *all the time!)*

I cannot even begin to tackle everything about male and female relationships in this

WHO ME? A LOVER?

book. Maybe someday you can help me with this subject. But I can't skip it altogether either.

Romantic relationships can develop into some beautiful and long-lasting friendships. (Lots of husbands and wives are best friends. Believe it or not!) But romantic relationships can also be just flashes, infatuations, dreamy and unreal crushes.

The romantic relationships that stand the best chance of succeeding are built on the following foundation:

- No masks. If somebody falls in love with your false front, what happens when the real you shows up?
- No games. "Macho man" and "bimbo" are games that nobody needs to play. Be yourself! If you are strong and decisive, be that way in a relationship. If you are really gentle and mushy, be that way.
- Sex is good. Sex is wonderful. But sex is not a game! Don't enter a relationship just for the pleasure of having sex with somebody. Nothing puts greater strings on a relationship than "Let's make love. No strings, baby!" Who is kidding whom?
- Communicate—about things that matter. Be honest and open in your communicating. If something seems wrong, talk about it.
- Be a friend. The key to success in any

romantic relationship is being a friend. That means no big *ifs,* no strings, just honest caring for the other person.

There are lots of mistakes to be made in romantic relationships. They are not easy. But remember, even in these relationships there can be healing, forgiveness, and second chances. (No matter your mistakes. You can be forgiven—you're worth it.)

Parents Count

"Father Don! If you are going to tell me I have to be friends with my parents, you might be going too far! I can't be buddy-buddy with them. I have tried. Honest."

It is very difficult to be *friends* with your parents during these teenage years. But loving your parents? That can happen.

Lots of parents hear rumors about the wonderful characteristics of their children—kind, loving, considerate, studious, courageous. Then they start to wonder if people are talking about the same blob in sneakers that hides in his or her room all day, grunts hello and good-bye, and is wired for sound twenty-four hours a day.

Before you start loving strangers, take a good look at your family—any family you have. It is easy to take families for granted. Most of the time family relationships seem like such a hassle.

WHO ME? A LOVER?

But I challenge you to try a new no-strings approach with your parents (and your whole family). You may have to change your image of your parents. You may have to stop looking at them as lawgivers and judges.

Try looking at your parents as people who care about you. Maybe if you change your image of your parents, you might be surprised at how unconditional their love for you has been all along!

But remember, they are still your parents. They are setting limits and guiding you—at least while you are in school and living at home. But if you want to grow into an adult friendship with the folks, you have to start changing the images now.

You have hurt your parents sometimes! (You can't get past puberty without doing that.) They have hurt you, too. (The frustrations of raising children makes the best of parents lash out at times.) But between parents and children there is always the chance for healing, forgiveness, and second chances. In fact, the love you practice at home with your family is a real laboratory for the loving you will need to do throughout your life. (Especially when you have children.)

Does God Count, Too?

Do you want friendship with God? Then it is yours for the asking. Loving God is very similar to loving friends. You need to spend time together. You need to want the relationship. You need to listen as well as talk. You need to work through the tough stuff.

How do you pray?

"Father Don, get real! I hardly ever pray. It just doesn't mean much. Are you telling me that *prayer* is part of friendship with God?"

Exactly! I'll bet you spend a lot of time asking God for good things and complaining about the bad things. Unless I miss my guess, when you *do* pray, you do all the talking. Jesus must be a pretty patient friend. If I were your best friend, I wouldn't stand for that.

In your relationship with God, shut up and listen. God is not known for loud messages. But God doesn't really whisper in your ear either. The Scriptures communicate God's Word. (I *really* hope you read that book someday.) But other signs of God are everywhere.

When you are talking and sharing with a friend, it's not the words that are so important. Just being together is the exciting part. Same with God—it isn't what you talk about that is so important. Just being together is what's exciting.

With any friendship, the first step is letting somebody in. You open up the door to yourself and let somebody get to know the real you. Same thing in a friendship with God—with Jesus. Let God in!

Nobody is forcing you. But it is worth the try. I would like you and God to become friends.

WHO ME? A LOVER?

But it is not any condition I have put on you. I am convinced that if you start loving without strings attached, if you give the gifts of healing, forgiveness, and a second chance to others, and if you pull off your mask and get real, you are going to find God. I can be patient. And I think you are in for a great surprise!

Don't Forget Yourself

I saved this one for last. Jesus summed up the whole law into two simple commandments: "Love God with your whole heart. Love your neighbor *as yourself.*" That must mean that you have to love yourself first. Once you know that you are lovable, you will be able to love others.

I am convinced that you are lovable. I am convinced that you have the ability to love others. I would stake my life on it! It may take you a while to wake up and face that yourself. It may not sink in right away. But someday you are going to be looking in the mirror. A big smile is going to come over your face—a real dumb grin. Then you will know the truth of it.

When you are standing there with toothpaste all over your mouth, remember all this stuff about unconditional love—love without strings. Then ask yourself, "Who me? A lover?"

You bet!

8

LET THE FUN BEGIN!

- I just knew you would get around to talking about church sooner or later.

- Is there any way I can party with church people and stay real?

- I would like to belong, but we don't have the same experiences—don't talk the same language.

- Let's hear it for the guitar player!

WHO'S GONNA LOVE ME?

What if I suggested that we take all this stuff about unconditional love and parties and healing and forgiveness and second chances, and move everything into the church? What if I suggested that church is a place where we can let the fun begin? What if I suggested that you can't do all this loving in a vacuum, so let's go to church?

"Here comes the real pitch! This is what Father Don was getting at all along. Herd 'em into church. Make 'em fall in line. How long has it been since this guy sat in church on a Sunday morning?"

Let's back up a few paces. I am not sure about just how you and church get along. You may be a regular. You may not have been to church in years. I am not too worried about that right now. I am sure that you need help being you. You do need a place to party. You do need the care and help of others who believe in you—who love you.

If I promised you that your parish church can offer you all those things *right now,* I might be blowing smoke. What I am telling you is that church is all about being together in love. Part of the problem with church is the old image bit again. People have an image of church—big building, pretty windows, moving liturgy, traditional hymns. This image tends to color how people relate to church.

If I think of church as "the house of God," I am going to picture a big building where God

LET THE FUN BEGIN!

dwells. It will be a holy place (probably set aside for the Judge, Boss, Scorekeeper God). If I think of church as an "institution," I will think of structures, bishops, priests, deacons, ministers, boards, synods—the whole bit. If I think of church as "teacher of the faithful," I might be concerned about doctrines, Bible study, moral teachings, true worship—sort of the watchdog of the truth.

None of these images is completely crazy. But if church is ever going to mean anything to you, you are going to have to get a new image for the church. I would like to give you two to think about. Okay?

- *People of God—people of love.* If you started thinking about church as a group of people gathered together to love God and to love one another, what pictures do you get? Do you get pictures of statues and pretty windows? Or—just maybe—do you get pictures of people getting together to cut some strings off their loving? Do you see people really trying to care for one another? Do you see people of all ages and colors and economic levels gathered together to praise God and support one another in life? (Amazing what getting a new image can do for you!)
- *Servant of all.* If you started to think of church as a group of people gathered

WHO'S GONNA LOVE ME?

together to take care of people's needs—physical, spiritual, emotional—what pictures do you get? Bingo and softball and catechism class? Popes and pageantry and potluck suppers? Or do you see a community of people who work together to make the whole world a better place to live?

I am not saying that church always lives up to those two images, but I didn't make them up. Those images come straight from the Bible. (I could tell you exactly where, but I am still hoping against hope that you will break down and read the Bible yourself. A hint: A guy named Paul wrote a lot of letters describing the church. Why not start there?)

Church may not be perfect (at all), but the church is for people.

> *Church Principle*
> *As a member of the church, you have the* right *to expect that your spiritual, physical, and emotional needs will be met. You have the* duty *to meet the spiritual, physical, and emotional needs of others.*

Right away you begin to see that belonging to the church needs some rethinking. You can't just slip into the old images and expect to get

LET THE FUN BEGIN!

the church thing right. But you are not the only one who needs to reimage the church.

PARTYING AT CHURCH

In a parish somewhere, a bunch of teenagers wanted to express their faith in the resurrection one Easter. They talked to the pastor and the worship committee. They got a spot right after Communion.

Everybody was settled down with their thoughts, when over the loudspeaker came a blast of (oh, no!) *rock and roll.* The teenagers played a song for the congregation that spoke to them of new life, hope, and joy! Rock and roll in church? Jaws went slack. Backs went up. But not a few toes started tapping. One elderly lady poked her husband and said, "It works for me!"

Not everybody liked the idea, but a new reality happened in that church. People saw for a moment that maybe, just maybe, these young people *did* have some faith. (If I told you the song was "40" by U2, could you figure out when this happened?)

But It's Boring!

I can't deny that church can be pretty boring. It hardly seems like a place to party. There is a *real* problem here. Music, ritual, sermons, prayers—

none of it seems to have anything to do with you.

Is it possible for you to celebrate your discovery of unconditional love in your parish (if you have a parish)? The answer is a definite maybe!

Honestly, I am not writing this book to push church at you. I don't want to put strings on God's love for you. (God will love you only if you participate in your parish. Skip church? No love!) But I am also convinced—because I have seen it happen—that you can find support for your loving and growing in church.

There are people who take time out to minister to young people. They are trying to listen to your concerns. They are trying to share what they believe in with you. They are trying to love you—without any strings.

But you need to speak up, too. Church might be boring because you have always expected it to be. You have never stood up and *asked* for the church to meet your concerns.

Don't get the idea that I think you should march in one Sunday, commandeer the sound system, and play rock and roll. You might make a point, but you will also rattle a few teeth.

What I am saying is that nobody is going to know your needs if you don't talk about them. Wouldn't it be great if you could walk into church one Sunday—really excited about the events of the week—and be able to celebrate what you're feeling? Wouldn't it be great if you

LET THE FUN BEGIN!

could look at the person sitting next to you and say, "You, too?" (there is a pun hiding there somewhere) and celebrate together? Well, I have this idea that just won't go away: Church could be like that.

BRIDGING THE GAPS

A lot of young people stand around and watch adults "do" church. Then they criticize the failures, or they drop out. The real challenge is to do something constructive. But to do something constructive, you have to get involved. ("See, I told you! He *is* pushing church!")

Now church leaders and pastors, adults and young people all have to overcome some real roadblocks to making church work. Basically, there are four big gaps that are at work between young people and adults when it comes to church. (These gaps exist almost everywhere in society, but for now I am sticking to church. What can it hurt?)

- *The relationship gap:* Some people call this the generation gap, but it happens with more than just teenagers and adults. A couple of questions will help you understand this gap. When you walk into church, who do you know? Who knows you? Who cares that you are there? Who is there that you care about? Did somebody greet you? Did you greet anybody? Did you see somebody that you want to talk with after church? The more people you know (and who know you) and care about (and who care about you), the better the experience of church will be. (Trust me on this one.)

- *The communications gap:* When you go to church, do you get a little fuzzy-headed? Do you feel that you are spending time on another planet? How do people communicate with you? What is the sermon about? What about the celebration? Is it clear? Has somebody explained what is going on? Are you expected to keep up—no questions asked? The more people try to keep everybody involved in liturgy, the better the experience of church will be.
- *The experience gap:* Not everybody in the church comes from the same place, does the same things, has the same feelings. Do you feel that nobody in church is paying attention to your needs? Are you concerned about the needs of other people? Do you get the feeling that this whole ceremony could rumble on without you? Do you feel that nobody is trying to reach out and touch you? Are you trying to reach out and touch anybody? The more the range

LET THE FUN BEGIN!

of human experience in the pews is touched, the better the experience of church will be.

- *The language gap:* This is a killer! It has to do with what I call "God-talk." It seems that the easiest way to talk to people about God is to use fancy theological language. (Not *thee*'s and *thou*'s so much—just that pious stuff that you don't understand.) Do you have to listen closely to make sure people are not praying in a foreign language? Do you hear a lot of words that just don't make any sense? Do the songs and prayers seem a million miles away from reality? Does the sermon seem to be about life on Mars? The closer the words of prayer and worship are to the everyday language of the people, the better the experience of church will be.

I have not solved the problem of church—but I am working on it. It won't happen right away. (Do you get the idea that this is sort of a theme in this book?) Not too long ago, somebody got the bright idea that if we got a guitar player to lead the singing, every teenager would come flocking back to church.

It was a simple solution, but it didn't work. Maybe the guitar music wasn't good enough. Maybe people just got tired. The idea was pretty good. The guitar music (at the very least) was an attempt to communicate with you—in language you could understand. The church is working at it—at least I think we are.

The most important thing is that you have the right to hear the words of love and life and hope and spirit in your language. Basically, that is why I do what I do. It is what Father Don is all about.

I hope you could understand this book. I hope you got the message that you are worthwhile. You are lovable. You are important.

What does old Father Don want from you? Just that you be the best you. I want you to become an unconditional lover—and I want you to feel that love without strings.

I am convinced that being a teenager is not a disease! You have a right to life! a right to love! a right to hope! a right to party!

Who Am I Gonna Love?

At the beginnig of this book, I told you I was going to talk about relationships—Jesse, Cindy, Roger, Mr. Sandstrom—all those wonderful people in the first story.

What was going on with Jesse anyway? Bet you can hardly remember. First of all, Jesse was dealing with the fear of rejection. He wanted Cindy to like him. He hated it when Roger made fun of him.

Jesse was afraid of pain, too. He didn't understand the deep hurt feelings he had. Jesse was frightened of failing. When Mr. Sandstrom caught him without his assignment, his failure was waved in front of the whole class. But most of all, Jesse was afraid of death. The suicide of a friend from grade school hit him right between the eyes.

WHO'S GONNA LOVE ME?

Jesse tried to follow the rules, but most of the rules were conditions for him being loved. He did not have a super opinion of himself. People loved him because he had a great stereo in his car.

I hope Jesse ran right out of that classroom and into the arms of some unconditional love. Maybe a parent, a teacher, a counselor, a coach—somebody who showed Jesse that it is possible to love without any strings attached. Then Jesse could heal that old self-image. He could forgive himself (and Roger and Cindy and Katy Albrite). He could start over!

I hope the same things for you—

- Love without strings
- Freedom from all those fears
- Healing
- Forgiveness
- A whole wagonload of second chances

Celebrate your life. Give yourself a break and be you—the best possible you.

Oh, just in case you missed the message, let me say it loud and clear (and without a single big *if*).

I love you!